Heaven's Call
to
Earthy Spirituality

D0888837

By
George McClendon

What do you say after you say goodbye?

First published by Dog Ear Publishing
4010 W. 86th Street, Ste H
Indianapolis, IN 46268
www.dogearpublishing.net

ISBN: 978-159858-703-6

This book is printed on acid-free paper.

Printed in the United States of America

Dedication

I dedicate this book

To my friends, clients, and students who have entrusted me with their life stories and have challenged me to shape my own.

To the monks, past and present, of St. Gregory's Abbey. They are my brothers.

To the women, Lady Dragons all, who have asked me that important question: "Who are you, really?"

To Bob and Mary Goulding, my mentors who helped me remember who I was.

To Ruth McClendon, who accompanied me into a new life and creativity.

To Claire Braz Valentine, my writing mentor, and to the weekly group who lovingly confronted me as I wrote.

To my brother Bob and my sister-in-law Marcy for their support.

To my wife Carol, who knows all my flaws and, in her own special way, still loves and encourages me.

To my daughters, Sarah and Jennifer, Gemini Twins, who doubly bless me as a father.

Table of Contents

Preface

"We must be still and still moving
Into another intensity
For a further union, a deeper communion"
                                    T.S. Eliot, *East Coker* lines 204ff

    Thomas Merton, monk and mystic, was a close friend of the Dalai Lama. After Merton died, the Dalai Lama remembered him as "his brother." Merton had been my spiritual guide even before I entered the monastic life. I read his book *Seven Storey Mountain* when I was in college, and it was pivotal in my decision to become a monk. In 1968, at a conference in Bangkok, he gave a talk to monks, Christian, Buddhist, and others, explaining his way of life. I quote from his *Asian Journal* some of his words that inspire the focus of my book:

> [The monk] is a marginal person who withdraws deliberately to the margin of society with a view to deepening fundamental human experience . . . I find myself representing perhaps hippies among you, poets, people of this kind who are seeking in all sorts of ways and have absolutely no established status whatever . . . The marginal person, the monk, the displaced person, the prisoner, all these people live in the presence of death, which calls into question the meaning of life... The office of the monk or the marginal person, the meditative person or the poet is to go beyond death even in this life, to go beyond the dichotomy of life and death and to be, therefore, a witness to life.

The great boxer, Mohammed Ali, used to say that he "floated like a butterfly and stung like a bee." At the margin, we temporarily abandon all the roles and all that define us. At the creative edge, we can be butterflies and bees. This is sacred space where we are present to better direct our consciousness.

As a marginal person, as one who lives on the edge of relevancy, I have written about my own life journey. Only in that place could I be creative. As I tell my story, I invite my readers to recall similar paths taken. I write about my childhood, years defined as a monk, discovery of an earthy spirituality and woman, good-bye to monastic life, and existence as a displaced person seeking sacred space in the world. Spiritual practice continues to be a thorough listening and life-changing integration of who I am in community.

I write in the first person, "I," to other marginal people, "we." We are many. We are those who do not fit well in marriages, family, the church, political parties, or other institutions. We are all in recovery of who we are. We are recovering from alcohol, drugs, divorces, and abuse. I write about how we have been defined by these relationships. We have learned to survive, protecting ourselves from rejection and abandonment.

We can let go, even as we experience the loneliness of our separation. We risk going to our edges because we know it is there that we can deepen ourselves and can become who we are. It is there that we embrace the paradoxes of life: faith and doubt, trust and fear, joy and sadness, and arrive at another place all together.

This book is about the practice of finding the just-right place when I/we have been displaced. The "just-right place" is one where we experience stability. It is a place where we are at home and know who we are. I also explore the practices of "thoroughly listening" and "radical change." These practices help us fine tune. We take in what we need to hear. We change (let go of) survivor ways that are no longer necessary as we creatively do our spiritual practice: finding our place, listening, and changing. We form a conspiracy of other seekers outside the box of relevancy. We support one another in that sacred space. We form a conspiracy, a community.

Introduction:
St. George and the Dragon Lady

On January 8, 1993, a client told me that she had dreamed of a man on a white horse doing battle with a dragon. It was the scene depicted by an icon of St. George and the Dragon that I keep in my counseling office. However, she said that she had never noticed the icon before, though I have had it displayed for quite some time. She asked me to explain what the icon meant, so I told her the story of St. George, the good knight, doing battle with evil, which is symbolized by the dragon. As I was telling this story, I felt she was distracted. She waited patiently until I finished and then said, "What is important to me is the cave or dark hole out of which the dragon emerges." I had owned that icon for nearly 30 years and had never noticed the hole in the earth that appears to be the dragon's source.

The George-Dragon battle is a Christian expression of the ancient Greek contest of Apollo, the sun god, and Python, the she-serpent. In that myth, the battle takes place at Delphi, where Python and a prophetic priestess serve Gaia, the Mother Goddess. Python dwells in the omphalos, a shrine built underground at Delphi. Apollo with his sun-arrows mortally wounds her.

Just as St. George meets his Dragon Lady at the mouth of the cave, I know that is the place to which I am called. There, I am in sacred space, the edge where George and Dragon meet. I write what I see and hear from the perspectives of George and Dragon.

Both inside themselves and between themselves, George and Dragon Lady need each other. Their relationship is the very essence of spiritual practice. Spirituality is steeped in the relationship of our opposites that often emerge from darkness. The spiritual task is to embrace our light and darkness, our masculine and feminine, our opposing archetypes. We listen to what they teach us and accept them as who we are. There is balance between George and the Dragon. Spirituality leads us to wholeness, not the elimination of parts. Avoiding our shadow side and calling that holiness does not create wholeness but rather fosters fragmentation. Spirituality, in the sense I am using it, seeks to integrate the shadow, along with the light, into the whole person.

It was not my original intention to focus on the male-female opposites, nor is it my intention to write a book on mythology. Authors such as Mircea Eliade and Joseph Campbell have done this in scholarly tomes. My intent is to use this particular depiction of George and the Dragon as a metaphor for what is possible. And what is possible is creative spirituality as integration, a spirituality of wholeness.

Without a deeper knowledge and acceptance of the relationship, struggle in the George-Dragon scene continues. It remains a story of "good" destroying "evil." I call this the "Survival Crisis," because it is often expressed in such statements as, "The way to survive is not to feel a certain feeling or express that feeling. The way to survive is not to be a certain way or simply not to be." Many of us have surrendered our individual spiritual paths because we do not want to be abandoned by our families, friends, lovers, and others. Spirituality that remains in the Survival Crisis is mired in patterns learned and practiced many times. Even when we say that we will not do it anymore, we find ourselves back in the George-Dragon struggle again. Having practiced so much, we know it very well!

I knew a man who had been sober for many years and who was very active in AA. I asked him who else he was besides an alcoholic. He answered that he had never thought about that. He also said it was frightening to think that way, because he might go back to drinking. He was St. George, who must always be prepared to ward off the Demon Rum. I hope that someday he will remember who was, and is, more than an alcoholic.

During a family gathering, I was describing the metaphor of George and Dragon to a relative. He understood the image but asked, "What happens when George is not killing dragons?"

I believe this is a pivotal question. What does George do during peacetime? Does he turn spears into plow shears? Does Dragon breathe fire when she is not being attacked? Do George and Dragon have another kind of relationship if they are not at war? How do they take care of themselves? Does George go off to a castle or a monastery to meditate and pray? Does he seek out his brother warriors? Does he have a lover, or is he celibate? Does he practice other virtues besides fortitude? Does he experiment with being more than a knight?

It is equally important to ask what Dragon does when not defending her safety. Does she go deep inside the cave to heal and dream about possible non-abusive relationships? Does she find peace there? Does she find her relationship to God there? Is her spirituality an earthy one, very different from George's more ethereal version? Does she experiment with the knowledge that her feelings are valuable, that she in her Dragon-ness is beautiful? Knowing that to be true, does she nurture the lovely maiden within her?

These places where George and Dragon go are cru-cial as preparation for what I call the "Creative Crisis." George and Dragon can retreat to their own places to pre-pare for another Survival Crisis.

They can arm themselves to ward off what each does not want, e.g., attack, rejection, criticism; or they can use this place to prepare for what they do want, e.g. peace, accep-tance, and praise. Those who have been abused can get ready for quality care. Those who were not allowed to be a child can get ready to experience the child that still lives inside them. Those who survived dysfunctional families can prepare themselves for a relationship that is supportive.

We have a choice between surviving in predictable, safe, familiar, and painful ways or moving forward to create or to co-create what is possible. What if George and Dragon created a safe place where they could do a different and new dance, one that honored George's penchant for riding horses and looking important and having lofty thoughts, while also embracing Dragon's need to stay close to the earth, feel deeply, and express those feelings to an understanding George? A new story about their intimacy would emerge. George would sometimes get off his "high horse" and approach the Dragon's cave. There he could listen to her, and she could see what that is like. She in turn could withhold her fire and climb up on his horse, to sense what the knightly life is like. She could listen and encourage him away from domi-nation. They would be on their way to finding a place where the "more" is possible.

I have plenty of experience of being on my own "high horse." I learned a long time ago that being "holy" is also quite lonely, even when in community with others who are "holy." The risk for me has been to come off my horse and view spirituality from the mouth of the cave.

Three Stages of Spiritual Life

A practitioner on a spiritual journey passes through thee stages: (l) <u>Defined by</u> the path, (2) <u>Separating from</u> the path, and (3) <u>Choosing or abandoning</u> the path. These stages may or may not be sequential. It isn't as if a seeker can say, once and for all, "I am no longer defined by or limited by the literal requirements of my practice. I have separated out and am free to choose from now on." We are, time and again, lapsing into a definition of who we are and what we do, being tempted to rest in that familiar, safe, and predictable place. To enliven our relationship to practice, just as we need to do in all relationships, we must separate enough to choose it. For example, marriage is a practice that can become a definition. We separate from it as a noun and make it an active participle, marrying, where we are, or are not, choosing our relationship. Any spiritual practice and practitioner faces the danger of becoming a noun defined by a noun.

I have borrowed from Hegel's philosophical concepts of "Thesis, Antithesis, Synthesis" to best describe the spiritual path. I have used this as a template for my story, my spiritual journey.

George the young monk.

Family in attendance at solemn vows.

Stage I: Thesis–Definition
George the Monk

It was July 10, 1953, a very hot day at St. Gregory's Abbey in Shawnee, Oklahoma. Clothed in the habit of a Benedictine monk, a novice, I felt very holy, not even noticing the heat. One of the monks remarked that if I lasted 'til next July, I certainly would notice the heat. My first contact with monasticism and the Benedictines was in the fall of 1947. As a young boy not yet 14, I left home and began my high school years in a boarding school run by the monks. The school had the same name as the Abbey, St. Gregory's, located on the prairie in Oklahoma not far from Oklahoma City. There is a story, told to me by one of the monks, that the Benedictines were on their way to California when some wagons broke down on the prairie. Rather than fix them, they decided to build where they were stranded.

The school motto was "builder of men," and we were known as the "knights of St. Gregory." After graduating from high school and spending a semester at a state college as a fraternity man, partier, and football player, I returned to St. Gregory's. I finished my first two years of college and became a monk in July of 1953.

The name given to me when I entered the monastery was George. As I knelt in the middle of the sanctuary after receiving the monastic habit, Abbot Philip said to me in Latin, "that in order to have a patron saint to guide you in your monastic life, you will be named George." I was to spend the next 25 years of my life as a monk.

It has taken me 40 years and an intervention from a woman client on January 10, 1993, to realize why I am George and how important that knowledge is to my spiritual life (Cf. Introduction). Because of her, I more fully understand the meaning of prayer. Spirituality and prayer are "earthwork." George comes from the Greek "gaia" (earth) and "ergon" (work). Realizing what my name means gives a better understanding of the Benedictine motto "Ora et Labora" "Pray and Work." Prayer and work are not to be separated, just as St. George and the Dragon coming from the hole in the earth must always be connected. Hole, Whole, and Holy are necessarily of the same spirit. I get myself in trouble when I sit perched on my white horse separated from the earth, separated from the hole out of which comes the juice of spirituality.

It is that dark, wet place from which your true prayer emerges. Its source is Gaia, the feminine from whom and with whom all birthing comes. Your prayer or meditation is a creative act, an art form — whole and holy — earthy spirituality.

For the first ten years of my monastic life, I had no idea of my deep need for the feminine. I felt very supported by the men, my brothers that surrounded me. The precepts of the Benedictine Rule guided me. I had a community to which I was attached as George McClendon of St. Gregory's Abbey.

During that time we were building our monastery and the refectory where we ate our meals. With the exception of a few skilled laborers, we did all the work ourselves. Needing room for the new construction, our first task was to move the monastic cemetery from the north side of the chapel to the south side. One monk was darkly humorous when he took Father Maurice's skull in his hands and quoted Shakespeare: "Alas poor Yorick…."

It seemed that prayer and work were never so clearly exemplified than during those years. Our lives were in balance. We were practicing the humility so very important in the life of a monk.

Prostrate before ordination

The spirit of the Rule for monks states that they need a place where they can be planted and well watered. The "I" and the "Thou" in community thrive much better when they are present in a rich, fertile context. The spiritual practice that makes this possible is humility. The word humility comes from the Latin root word "humus" meaning "earth" or "soil." Your practice of humility entails returning to the earth part of yourself. It helps to remember the maxim: "you are dust and to dust you will return." This returning process demands that you die to inflated parts of self that take you away from your grounding. Ego and narcissism are out of touch with earthiness. Humility is the ground for community.

We were close to the earth, and we provided each other with many opportunities to be humble. Father John, my football coach when I attended the boarding school staffed by the monks, was in charge of our building projects. I can still

Ordination to the Priesthood

hear his voice as he called my name to do something. It was just like being back on the football team! "Mac, get in there and stop that quarterback- -George, get in there and carry that bag of cement!" We worked together and prayed together. Abbot Philip, our monastic leader, was digging ditches right next to the young monks. This was the middle or balanced way to the Benedictines. Though there were many burdens attached to living in community, I had a deep sense that this was sacred space, a holy place, where others on the same path as I were seekers.

Father's family

Mother:Lela, and George

Grandpa:Weaver, Father: Earl, and George

Early Earthy Spirituality

A child, in beginning years, the first five, receives many epiphanies of sacred presence: a mother's smile, a cat or dog that accepts and gives attention, a sunrise or sunset, a stone, a toy. There is only a thin curtain between the material world and the spiritual for the child. Maybe they remember the connection because they are only recently separated from an intimacy where all is one. Children resonate with awe and wonder to these events during a time in life, though brief, when control, conflict, and compliance are not survival issues, a time before the ego has developed layers distancing the child from events. Experiences are— the child is, not in a separate but a mystical and unitative presence.

As children mature, understand boundaries, and learn how to survive, they forget that they are natural contemplatives, not separate as subjects to objects. As we get older, we become complex. The word comes from the Latin: com-plexus meaning <u>with folds</u>. The Latin for simple is symplexus meaning <u>without folds</u>. Folds insulate and prevent creativity. Some, as adults, by various spiritual practices, let go of the complexities—control, conflict, compliance—and recapture what came to them <u>simply</u> as children. "I assure you, unless you change, and become like little children, you will not enter the kingdom of God." (Mt 18:3)

Merton speaks of Contemplation in these words: "Contemplation goes beyond concepts and apprehends God not as a separate object but as the Reality within our reality, the Being within our being, the life of our life."

My first five years of life continue to influence me today. I was fortunate, blessed, and made special; not the case with those rejected, abandoned, and abused early in life. As a psychotherapist, I have visited those terrible years with clients who learned to survive in hell instead of thriving in sacred space.

I was not the firstborn. Doris Ann was a sister, an infant with a defective heart who died a year before my birth. I remember hearing how my father and mother tried to keep her alive and finally let her go. I believe they mourned her death and decided to have another baby as soon as possible.

I was born on November 10, 1933, in Okmulgee, Oklahoma. Okmulgee is the Creek Indian Nation capital and is located near Tulsa. The Great Depression was underway, and Oklahoma was the Dust Bowl, *Grapes of Wrath* country. My parents were especially careful with me as a baby, they feared losing me as well. They fed me according to childcare books of the time, and yet I continually cried. They took me to our local physician, Doctor Edwards, who, after an examination, said: "There's nothing wrong with this boy. He's just hungry. Feed him!" That became the story of my life. When I am hungry, I want to be fed. I simply need to know what it is for which I hunger. I cannot eat or drink enough to fill up an intimacy hunger or spiritual hunger. For what do you hunger or thirst?

We were poor. Our home did not have electricity. Our light came from coal oil lamps; we drew our water by a hand pump from a well in the backyard, and we had an outhouse farther away. Though we did not have much, I consider the first five years of my life to be among the happiest. I invite you to remember your first five years. If you have photos of yourself, look at them, see who you are and what you feel. Remember!

The following are some of my cyclical time events in which I left the ordinary, entered sacred time, and returned to ordinary time. Though they happened long ago, they are very much present to the little boy still inside this 74-year-old man. These are crucial in every person's journey. I think of them as mysteries because they have meaning far beyond the rational explanation given the events. They took place before the age of reason, not filtered through consciousness, but were events evoking Presence. The little boy reverberated to that Presence and resonated from an uncomplicated place within.

One of the most unforgettable mysteries—and perhaps my earliest memory—is an Andrew Wyeth scene where my mother sits in a rocking chair with me on her lap. The curtains are blowing with typical Oklahoma wind and she is singing: "She'll be comin' 'round the mountain when she comes....She'll be drivin' six white horses when she comes." All is well, and all is secure. I am two or three years old.

When I am three or four, I am in our living room. The Bible is open upon the table in front of a window, facing west. The sun is setting, the sky a bright red. The picture in the Bible matches the sky before me. I believe I made a connection between beauty and spirituality in that instant.

One holiday I ask my Grandpa, Weaver, why we eat cranberry sauce at Thanksgiving. He answers, "So we could eat more turkey." This made sense to me. My Grandpa knew those practical things in life. He was the wise man who later told me not to spit into the wind and not to pee uphill. These words of advice have served me well all my life.

This is the time when Agnes Erman and I have our first "sexual" experience, exploring each other's body under my parents' bed. It is an exciting and curious venture that no parent discovers and judges to be wrong. At about seven, after we move to town, I did get such a message while playing "doctor" with Mary Ann Cunningham in the swing on our front porch.

I love digging potatoes out of the ground in our garden, where we raise much of our own food. I am fascinated as I watch my dad wring the neck of a chicken, pluck its feathers, and bring it inside the house or leave it outside where my mother cooks it in a pot.

These are earthy times for that little boy. They are a foreshadowing to the earthy spirituality to which I am called many years later. I cherish those years spent living in that old house on a country road in Okmulgee until, at five, we move to town, and my brother is born. Loved so much and deeply nourished, there is a reserve to draw upon as I get older and times are not so joyful.

St. Gregory's college

St. Gregory's monastery

Sacred and Ordinary Place
George and the Dragon
To Whom Much Has Been Given...

Everyone has been in sacred time and in sacred place of deep awe and wonder. We realize for the first time how profoundly someone loves us and how much we love someone. Maybe we experience it at a birth or death or, for the first time, we experience how beautiful a sunset is. Such events can change our lives. This comes with an expectation: "To whom much has been given, much will be required." Grudgingly returning to the ordinary world, we do our best to remember what happened when we were surrounded by the sacred and look for ways to introduce the experience into our daily lives. Meditation, spiritual, and religious rituals are, at their best, ways to re-present luminous mystical events. Having opened up to the possibility, many believe they must return to that place and time of gifting. There is a saying that if you have gone to the mountaintop and do not return, it is better that you had not gone at all. Our way of life and spiritual practices remind us of who we are and to what we are called.

The monastery was a place where I could pass through the gate from the ordinary, enter the sacred, and return smoothly to the ordinary. Of the vows made as a monk, the most important was that of Stability. It meant that I had a monastery, to which I was attached, as George McClendon of St. Gregory's Abbey. It was a place of reference for me no matter where I traveled. As a member of that particular community, in that particular place, never lost, I had no trouble locating myself.

Place informed other areas of monastic life. One assumed his "place" according to the time that he entered the community. The younger monks stood in the lower choir stalls where the monks gathered for prayer. "Younger" meant the most recent members. The "older" monks stood and prayed in the higher choir stalls or the ones in the rear. Even as we lined up for prayer or meals in "statio" (standing place), the younger monks would stand and walk in front; the elders would follow behind.

This sense of order pervaded our daily lives. There was a specific time to rise in the morning for prayer. Prayers were prayed every day at set times. Meals were eaten at regular times, and night silence began after night prayer. Each season of the church year dictated which parts of Scripture were used in our prayers. This order gave me a sense of security.

When I left the monastery in 1971, I no longer had the support of my community, my brothers, in this pursuit. I abandoned the sacred practices of common prayer, meditative silence, rich ceremonial rituals, and 20-plus years of stability. For six years after leaving, depressed and displaced, I worked, drank, and ate too much, attempting to fill up empty spaces.

From the late 70s til the present, I have found a new way of life with stability and balance enough to support my practice. Here and now is my stability. I do my practice from this place.

How have you lost your place? Are you in the process of finding a new stability in your life?

Outside monastic life, we need to support one another as we prepare to make much MORE possible. Our task is to find the "just-right place." You will remember that Goldilocks was looking for the "just-right" when she visited the home of the three bears: the soup was too hot, too cold, and just right. The bed was too hard, too soft, and just right. Finding and preparing the "just-right place" is crucial before engaging in communication or problem solving. It is necessary before prayer and meditation. Dogs and cats can teach us something about the "just-right place" as they sometimes circle about until they find where they need to be. There, they observe or sleep.

We need to learn to get ready. Sometimes we lack the sensitivity needed to locate the "just-right place." We abandon stability and are obsessed with productivity and problem solving. In our doing, we forget how and where to be.

As a business manager for a small college, I submitted a budget at a board meeting. Our board consisted mostly of successful businessmen. Before we sat down to address the budget, it seemed to me and to the president of the college that these men were wasting precious time chitchatting about sports and their families instead of getting down to "business." After what seemed a long time, they did sit down and quite rapidly discussed and approved the budget. I realized that through their personal, preliminary sharing, they were forming a place of connection from which they might more easily reach consensus.

I took my family to see the Barnum and Bailey Circus. The Ponzo brothers performed a high-wire act. One of the brothers perched on a unicycle atop a platform high in the air, another brother sat on his shoulders; and yet another perched on the second brother's shoulders. This third brother held a long balancing pole. The object was to cross from one platform to another on a thin wire. I was most impressed with how carefully they achieved their balance. This just-right balance seemed to be the focus of most of their act. Once achieved and at the just-right moment, they crossed the wire in no time at all. The crossing was almost anticlimatic to the preparation.

What is your preparation to be ready? Do you give yourself all the time you need to get balanced?

I was in a nine-month course on Spiritual Direction. During that period the location had to be changed four times due to parking, rental, and financial problems. Through this ordeal I learned something about different ways of solving problems. Thirty or so of the students in the program were women, and three students were men. As a man I felt a strong urge to suggest we go and get a place. Just solve the problem and end the struggle! If I had been the director of the institute, I would have pushed in that direction. Instead, I witnessed and found myself joining the women who shared their feelings of disappointment and angst at our continuing upheaval. I noticed that through this process we formed a place of stability, a psychological bond even though we were pilgrims without a home. What a difference it made to solve the problem of the physical setting from a place where we were one community.

Sometimes when we have a place for us, we lose it and have to find it again. Finding our place after we lose it is a challenge. The way to find it is to make sure that the sacred is all around us, so that we can at all times reach out and reconnect to it. We need to save our relationship by a touch, a look, a note, a gift, or other manifestations, so that we know it is alive and well even though we lost it momentarily. As I am typing these words on my computer, every 15 minutes a reminder appears on my screen asking me if I want to save what I have created. I have had the experience of losing some of my work because I didn't save it. We need to protect the precious moments of our relationships so that when we lose our place, we can find it again.

A man described to me a condition he faces in his life. He suffers from arthritis that shows up as stiffness in his back, and he has a medical problem in his knees brought on by the type of work he does. His ordinary way to deal with his pain and stiffness is to do nothing or, on the other hand, to force himself to push through his pain, causing more damage to his body. His task, now that he has gotten much worse and is in the care of a physical therapist, is to find a place in his exercise and activity where he does just enough to stretch his muscles without over-extending, and yet still exercise. This is the "just-right place" where he has a chance of healing. To do this practice, he must not do too much or too little.

This is a place of balance! Similarly in spiritual practice, we need to find the place where we can stretch ourselves. This stretching takes the form of experimenting with new behaviors that are not too familiar, predictable, safe, and painful. This is the edge where we can push boundaries and risk that we can create something new, surprising, risky, and pleasurable. This is the place where we have the opportunity to heal damage we have done. We condition ourselves for the possible.

Thoroughly Listening—George and Dragon Listen with Their Hearts

*"Listen carefully, my son, to the master's instructions,
and attend to them with the ear of your heart."*
Prologue—The Rule of St. Benedict

A second vow I made as a Benedictine monk was Obedience.

Too often this vow has been misconstrued. Obedience derives from the Latin words "ob" (thoroughly) and "audire" (to listen). Obedience, then, means to "thoroughly listen." What a difference it makes if we re-translate the standard marriage vows as Love, Honor, and Thoroughly Listen to Each Other.

Once we have found our place, we simply listen! Native Americans, as part of the training for a young brave, require that the boy go off by himself to a place where he can learn to listen when there is no sound, to see when there is nothing visible, to detect scents when there is nothing to smell, or to taste when there is nothing for the palate. Another practice is the vision quest. A person at important times in life goes to a special place and fasts while waiting and listening for the vision and words that the spiritual guides provide.

As a monk, I learned to obey (listen to) the Abbot, the father figure in the monastery. He, in turn was encouraged, by St. Benedict's rule for monks, to listen to the special needs of the community and lead them with firmness and compassion.

We spent a considerable portion of our days in silence. We ate our meals in the refectory, dining hall, which was outfitted with long tables on both sides of the room. The abbot's table was in front and a podium or pulpit from which one of the monks, as lector, read to us during the midday meal and at supper. The readings mostly were of a spiritual nature, but often included history or books of general interest. It is amazing how many tomes we digested as we ate our meals in silence. Humor found its way into our mealtimes when the lector, often a young monk, would misread a passage or mispronounce a word. From the *Martyrology*, a history of saints who died defending their faith, we heard: "St. Aurelius (?) gave up his life upon a flaming brassiere." He misread "brazier." A roar of laughter rising from silent monks filled the refectory!

We were silent following our final night prayer, Compline, until after breakfast the next morning. Night silence was a wonderful time to listen to our hearts and thoughts, read, and rest. Today, I still practice silence during early morning hours when I am the only one awake in my home. I meditate, read, and write—a great time to thoroughly listen. It is a time for deeper consciousness without the distractions of yesterday and the day before me.

Even for those who live alone, it is an opportunity to go deep inside, visiting the difference between being lonely and being all one. Sometimes you may forget to affirm your integrity in the midst of the fragmentations of the day.

There are three levels of listening: (1) the literal level, (2) the metaphorical level, and (3) the paradoxical level.

Literal Level

When we prepare to practice literal listening, we establish a place of acceptance in ourselves. We open to what is happening right now, right here. Sometimes this is the most difficult of all practices. Our challenge is to listen thoroughly with our whole body to our pain, addictions, talents, and successes, to what we feel, think, want, and need, and to who we are. Buddhists describe this process as "mindfulness."

What have you not listened to before because you have been too frightened, sad, or angry, assuming so much about others and yourself? What if you act as if you did not know others or yourself so well and open up pathways to new information, bad and good? This is an opportunity to practice awe and wonder, listening in the childlike way you and I did before we learned not to.

Metaphorical Level

We need to dream more, tell our stories, dance, write, expose ourselves to poetry and music; to create rituals that spell out and symbolize our relationships; to experience our lives as comedy and tragedy. This level of attending is crucial to making new decisions possible. We can, after thoroughly listening to one another in this context, say: "Maybe there is a place for us after all."

Gregory Bateson, one of my mentors, was a real master of the metaphor. He said, "Man's reach should exceed his grasp, or, what's a meta phor?" And, "Neurotics need to dream more, and psychotics need to know the difference."

Bateson once suggested I explore the connection between the bonsai tree and a Japanese-American family. I contacted the president of the local bonsai society and was invited to his home, where I viewed his trees and his family in that context. The way they cared for their family was artistically represented in their bonsais. Their sense of order and respect was reflected in the shape of the trees and care given them. I learned far more about this particular family by experiencing them through bonsai as metaphor than through a conventional interview approach.

In my therapy practice, I often invite clients to sing their problems to each other.

Imagine the effect of hearing your partner singing to you while borrowing from opera, country and western, or today's rap mode: "When you come home drunk, don't make love to me or take out the garbage when you say you will, I'm hurt, sad, and angry—so hurt sad, and angry!" Putting our problems and feelings to verse or song helps us hear the

More. *We have widened and deepened our perspective. This method does not discount the problems we experience. We simply reframe them. Individuals often laugh while singing or being sung to. This is not laughter at something that is not funny (gallows laughter), but laughter when More is created. We laugh as an audience at Laurel and Hardy pushing a piano up a hill because we, from our perspective, see that there is a much simpler way to move the piano. This way is outside their frame but is evident to us in the larger context.*

Metaphor increases the frame where we muster the most and best of ourselves to deal with the problems we face. We lose precious contact within ourselves and with each other when we stop dreaming, experiencing visions, or having fantasies. In other words, we are only listening to the literal in our lives.

Acting as if also provides the larger context.

Once I was counseling a couple who were having sexual problems because the man kept seeing his mother at the foot of their bed while he and his mate were making love. Because of this vision, he was unable to have an erection. In this instance, it was very important for us to remove an "as if" (his mother) from the bedroom and to create a new "as if." We decided to do an exorcism! Replete with make-believe candles and music, we had a procession in which we ushered Mother out of the bedroom and closed the door after telling her that she had no place there. This was their place to do whatever they wanted. After dealing with some of the literal messages he had received about sexuality, he, from this new place of listening, made a new decision. They reported back to me that his mother was no longer at the foot of their bed!

Every person has the capacity to evoke the More through metaphor. We sometimes need to challenge our literalness. Too often, because we are rewarded as problem solvers at work, home, or school, we apply similar techniques to our lives. By so doing, we deprive ourselves of places of deeper listening. To attempt to solve problems from the literal place only, without the support of metaphor, makes our relating to life too much like work. If we listen to our metaphors, we might recapture our sacred place, where there is mystery and where magic happens.

In order to listen to the More of that which resonates between us, we need to increase our frame of reference encompassing the possibilities.

Paradoxical Level

This third level of thoroughly listening, the Paradoxical, requires flexibility beyond the literal or the metaphorical. It asks that we be balanced and supportive of one another as we practice embracing the paradoxes in our lives. Gregory Bateson defined a paradox as "a set of opposites, in which case we choose both." This definition contains two crucial elements that increase our listening. Our culture tends to negate the experience of opposites. We have a very low tolerance for holding opposites and the tension they create. Our way is to choose one or the other: "Either you love me or leave me." "Either comply or rebel." "Either live or die." "Either be close or distant." "Either grow up or be a child." "Either be a girl or a boy." "Either be or not be." We learn that certain sets of feelings are not acceptable: "Either you feel what you feel, or you feel what I feel." This, of course, is crazy making, another form of "I'm cold, put on your jacket." Messages (injunctions) such as these place the receiver in a double bind. If I put on my jacket to please my partner, or to keep my partner from becoming angry, hurt, or depressed, I may have to discount my own body temperature or needs. If I choose to honor my own needs, I will not respect the needs of my partner. "In this town (home), there is not room for both of us." We learned to survive by choosing one of the set opposites, thereby complying or rebelling at a cost to self or other.

Self and other are the ultimate paradox for which we must make room. The second part of Bateson's definition is crucial at this juncture: "in which case we choose both." Is it possible in this relationship to, first of all, thoroughly listen to myself and to you? Then is it possible to listen and respond to the opposites that exist in me and in you? For example, is it possible to listen to myself when the message is, "I love you, and I hate you?"

Can I authentically listen to and embrace the fact that you might love me and hate me at the same time, or want to be close to me and be away from me? I have found that if my clients in therapy accept these opposites in themselves first, then it is easier to accept them in their partners. Instead of "either-or," our task is to attune to the place of the "both-and." Our practice here is to listen and hold both at the same time. We can do this everyday as we listen to pleasure-pain, excitement-fear, joy- sadness, softness-hardness, etc. Note that it is not just a matter of enduring both polarities; it means that we choose both. By attending to both at the same, holding them, balanced, we move forward.

I have learned something about this in my practice of running. When I run a long distance, such as a marathon, I know I will confront the pleasure- pain opposites. It is precisely at that point, when I meet the "wall" at mile 18 or so that I must attend to the opposites. I must remind myself that I have completed most of the race and that I can finish. I must also acknowledge the pain I am experiencing. I would be foolish to ignore pain that signals injury, and it is equally important to listen to the pain that accompanies the pleasure of performing such a test of endurance. Any mother who has given birth to a child can verify the pleasure-pain set that goes with this beautiful event!

Pleasure is not pain, love is not hate, living is not dying, and joy is not sadness. There is an "in between" the two that we can discover when we hold both. We can create something very beautiful from that place!

Once I was counseling a family with a mother, father,

and a six- year- old boy. During the session, the little boy crawled behind the couch on which the family was sitting. He began to amuse himself by adjusting the blinds that covered a window behind the couch. After listening to the racket for a while, the father disciplined his son. The boy cried out, "I hate you!" and stopped the distraction. Later on during the session, the boy climbed onto the father's lap, and the father held his son, showing affection to him, and the boy relished in it. I, at that point, interrupted the session to note with this family how blessed they were to have created such a place of security in which it was possible to express both hate and love.

We thoroughly listen to the "more" by focusing on that which is paradoxical. "Obedience" to these rich resources gives us more to work with as we reach out for what is possible. Without attending to these places, we will be trapped by what we think is going on. We will try to solve problems, losing the richness, the music, the color, the fragrance, and meaning of it all. We could miss the comedies and the tragedies that so enrich our lives, the metaphors of the divine.

Conversion

You have tasted sacred space and sacred time, learned to listen to the spirit speaking to you about beauty, truth, love and balance. Now continue your life's work: change!

The third vow I made as a Benedictine monk was that of Conversatio Morum. Its translation implies complete life change. Greek language has a word, "metanoia," best approaching the meaning: complete change from the inside out. The first vow, stability, places the monk in a particular location. The second vow, obedience, requires thorough listening, deep consciousness. And the third vow, conversatio morum, conversion, spiritual alignment.

As a Benedictine monk, I lived in community. The close relationship with these men helped mold me, year after year, just as a marriage or a close intimate relationship does with lovers. There were not many places within the monastery where a monk could hide. I could isolate myself in my cell for a while, but if I was not in my place with the rest of the monks or wasn't performing my assigned duties, someone would wonder where George was and would check and see if I was ok.

They were my brothers, and I was theirs.

We committed to live with one another and deal with our idiosyncrasies and problems. This is an earthy definition of monasticism: You live in your cell next to a monk who is difficult to endure. He snores loudly, doesn't clean his cell, or doesn't bathe very often. Finally, after 20 years, he dies. Then someone just as unbearable moves into the cell next to you. That's monasticism! The relationship rubs, both positive and negative, were an important part of my conversion.

Another element in my change and my growth, were my failures. We monks strove to be spiritual athletes. Seeking perfection as a monk meant that I had ample opportunities to practice humility in my pursuit of excellence. Thank God, I had an Abbot and wise brother monks who reminded me of another description of monasticism: "You fall down and you get up, you fall down and you get up."

You may have made a radical life change letting go of that which has tethered you. It may have been the end of a relationship to a person, a profession, or an addiction. It may have been the time when, as they teach in AA, you were "sick and tired of being sick and tired;" saying "no" to living a life that is familiar, predictable, safe, and painful. Some remember the exact day and hour of that decision. You began the process of recovering your own identity and feelings. It was the time when, no longer protecting yourself from what you did not want, you opened to an abundance of permission, protection, and power to seek what was possible.

You and I have been given simple, not easy, directives: Enter sacred space, listen, and change! We continue conversion, change, as a practice. Conversion becomes a participle instead of a noun. We are <u>converting</u> our lives for the rest of our lives. This practice is similar to that of the marriage vows. Marriage can become "wedlock" unless we continue to marry our spouse. Partners enter the sacred space of their love, listening to each other and changing. My wife says to me, "Don't tell me you are sorry. Change!"

On our spiritual journey, we sometimes lose our place; find it, listen, and change. The monk falls down, gets up, falls down, and gets up. This is the practice. All we have to do is change our path to align with what we have learned. It is another opportunity to listen. When I use the word "hear" or "listen," I mean what we attend with all our senses and emotions. They tell us, if we are tuned to them, what we need to do.

I had a client who was a paramedic. He explained to me how important it was, when he came upon an emergency, for him to pause, assess the situation, and, only then, act. *You and I flail about when we do not know what to do and are not listening to what is needed. We lose our place. Meditation and prayer are ways to find it again. In meditation, we follow our breath as it leads us to our creative edge or margin. We wait there and listen. Sometimes we may hear in our heart what we need to hear. Sometimes we have mystical experiences in which we let go of believing something to be true; we simply know it is so. At other times, nothing happens, and we continue to meditate and pray.*

A motto for Benedictine monasticism is "Ora et Labora." Pray and Work. We monks did manual labor and teaching. Some of the monks were artists, some were carpenters or poets. It was at our creative edge that we converted our lives. Our task was to bring mindfulness and good intention to our work, so that what we did had meaning and purpose beyond self serving motives. There is a Benedictine motto: "Ut in omnia glorificetur deus." That in all things God may be glorified. Our work was a form of prayer. St. Benedict asks that monks treat their tools as if they were vessels of the altar

Continue to hone your intentions. By this practice, ordinary work becomes sacred. When it comes time to meditate or pray, the transition is easier. You change to be in tune. This is "at-one-ment," atonement. Internal and external life change on a personal level becomes a template for a deeper consciousness shared in the communities in which we live. Your work becomes your prayer and your prayer, your work. In monasticism it is called "Opus Dei," the work of God.

George:Priest

Stage II: Antithesis--
Separation
Earthy Spirituality

There comes a time in your life, just as it did in mine, when you come to an important crossroad, a "Crisis" which can be defined as a turning point. We can attempt to continue on a familiar path or change our lives. It is a "dangerous opportunity."

I ran the Big Sir Marathon in 1990. The race begins in Big Sur and terminates at Carmel, California. The route follows the Pacific coast, presenting beautiful vistas of sea, cliffs, and mountains. As I was running along a fairly flat area that began to stretch abruptly upwards, an older woman wearing black tennis shoes ran past me. As she passed she yelled, "Another f...ing mountain!" This was a crisis on our 26 mile journey.

In the late 60s, I thought I knew how to live my life. I knew who I was: George, celibate monk and priest. Then, as the woman said, I was faced with another "f...ing mountain" that was to change my life.

As I write about my crisis, I invite you to examine the time, or times, in your life when you have faced dangerous opportunities and what choices you have made.

Touched by the Dragon

Bob & Carol & Ted & Alice was a 1969 movie depicting sensitivity groups at Esalon, a mecca for change along the Big Sur Coast in California. Though I wasn't ready for the sexual aspects of the movie, I was curious about group therapy. The Episcopal Church was sponsoring a workshop on sensitivity training at Oklahoma University. Surely Episcopalians would not be dangerous! So I went. One of our assignments was to prepare a collage of pictures and texts we cut from various magazines. These were supposed to represent something about us. Once we pasted them onto a piece of cardboard, we were to introduce ourselves using what we created. Nervously, I waited my turn in the circle as we sat together on the floor.

"I am Father George" I said, my voice quivering as I held my collage for all to see. I don't remember whether my pictures and text supported my declaration, nor do I remember if I was wearing my clerical collar.

"Who are you really?" a woman in the group asked. It was in the late 1960s.

The assassinations of John and Bobby Kennedy and Martin Luther King touched us, as it did everyone. I became active outside the walls of my monastery as we in religious life were going through a profound change. Pope John XXIII had convened a council of the Catholic Church with the goal of modernizing who we were. I was a monk and priest, and along with others of my profession was experimenting with what it meant to be relevant in modern times. There is an old saying in monasticism that the "habit does not make the monk." Monks and nuns began to set aside their habits and entered into more direct contact with the world. Who were we in this context?

Who was I really? Never had I been asked that question. My familiar, predictable, safe, and painful response, "I am a monk of St. Gregory's Abbey," would not suffice. This was sensitivity training. Good God, they were asking me to feel, to touch, and to be touched! Blindfolded, I was led to a tree. I touched it, the texture of the bark, edges, softness, firmness, the in-between spaces, the ups and downs. That was it! I became a feeler.

"Who are you?"

"I am a man who feels."

The Abbot asked me to go to the university and get a

masters in business administration. I, as an obedient monk, did this while studying spirituality and psychology during the summer breaks. Perhaps the Abbot of the monastery, feeling guilty about feeding me to the lions of economic relevancy, granted me freedom to pursue these studies. After I finished my MBA, I became business manager of the small college we Benedictine monks staffed.

For balance and for my own sanity, I also became chaplain for the college. Eventually I opened a center supporting students struggling with the 60s drug culture. The center's purpose was to help young people deal with emotional and spiritual problems. This became a place for me also, because I soon met someone who was to be my earth woman, teaching me more about sensuality and sexuality.

I invite the reader to understand that I, until my late 30s, I was a virgin. I had maintained my celibacy as a monk and priest by practicing strict avoidance. This was the definition of my disembodied spirituality, and I was good at it. I, along with my community of other celibates, was a spiritual athlete. We worked and prayed together and supported each other in our personal battles with the world flesh and the devil. We were obedient to the Father, or Abbot. We were like knights of King Arthur's court. Then came the 60s, sensitivity, and involvement.

I never resisted anything so much in all my life. My lover and I had intercourse about spiritual matters, which I could do comfortably, and had sexual intercourse, which I could only do awkwardly. She was my teacher, and I was not a good student.

I went outside those safe walls of the monastery and escaped back to them when I felt too threatened by my intense feminine contact. It wasn't so much sexuality as such, but the abundance of touch and closeness that penetrated my pores and my heart. I would not let myself simply savor the richness of it all, but would feel guilty, withdraw from her, promise that I would not do it again, then return to her. Because I was not patient with myself, I wouldn't accept her patience with me. I knew how to deal with what was difficult such as scarcity and deprivation, not with what was soft, accepting, and abundant.

I struggled with the feminine energy that she poured into our relationship and was not prepared for such earthy sensuality. I can best explain what happened by using mythical language. I experienced the undulatory energy (chi) possessed by the she-dragon, Python. This energy rests at the base of the spine until awakened. It is called the kundalini, or serpent power. Intimacy awakened me in a way I had never known. I had no experience with that kind of love. This called for an availability that I am only now beginning to accept and nurture. I was truly a novice in 1970 when I was 37 years old.

Python guarded the ancient Greek shrine of Delphi where Gaia, the earth mother, took her abode. In mythical times, Apollo attempted to destroy the power of Gaia. The God Apollo killed Python and turned the focus away from a Goddess society to a Patriarchal one. It is interesting that the name given me when I entered the monastery was George. The Christian equivalent of Apollo, George killed dragons that threatened early communities of believers. For me, instead of killing Python, as the song goes, She was "killing me softly" with her love.

I was going through radical changes in my life, becoming a popular priest in the local parish. The people supported my work, and I was receiving that kind of support for the first time. I was in a very rapid transition from being a humble monk to being a local celebrity. My name appeared in the newspaper, and I had a radio show. People attended the mass that I conducted on Sundays and praised me for my sermons. During this time I was chosen, along with Oral Roberts, a popular evangelist, to give the prayer at the inauguration of Oklahoma's new governor.

All this was like rich wine, and I was becoming intoxicated. Not prepared to assimilate such adulation, I began to drink more alcohol to deaden and make palatable all the richness of her love and the attention. I vacillated between excitement and guilt. Sometimes I would tell her that we could not see each other anymore. Other times, wanting to be with her, I sought her out, spent time together, felt guilty, went to confession, reached out again.

I was lost. I did not know how to encompass all that was happening in my life, feeling the hubris of it all, and was depressed at the same time. I had eaten of the apple and was approaching a form of freedom that I had never known. I had experienced my Garden of Eden in the monastery where I was safe and choices were made for me. All I needed was to be obedient. Now, She and I had begun a journey that was no longer familiar, predictable, nor safe.

John Milton, at the end of *Paradise Lost*, describes the place to which She and I had come:

"In either hand the hast'ning Angel caught
Our ling'ring Parents, and to th' Eastern Gate
Led them direct, and down the Cliff as fast
To the subjected Plain; then disappear'd
They looking back, all th' Eastern side beheld
Of Paradise, so late their happy seat,
Wav'd over by that flaming Brand, the Gate
The World was all before them, where to choose
Thir place of rest, and Providence thir guide:
They hand in hand with wand'ring steps and slow,
Through Eden took thir solitary way."

There is a saying that people having love affairs should never play in their own back yard. I was naive and did not know the rules. I managed not to think about the danger. Many helped me leave my "Garden of Eden." Spies watched what their priest was doing, and the pastor of the parish warned me. I was convicted of wrongdoing. In a way, I felt relieved that I no longer needed to lead such a secret life. The Abbot, to avoid scandal, decided that I should be assigned to a parish in East Los Angeles. I felt that I was being sent into exile, which also was to be a gift in disguise. It was, as I look back, an opportunity to regain my "paradisiacal" dignity. Once I found my perspective, I realized then, as I do now, how much she meant to me. She was my Python, my beloved Dragon Lady.

About two or three years later, after I had moved to the Monterey Bay area, she called to ask if I would ever return to her and our relationship. I said I would not. Later I heard that she had married. The governor whom Oral Roberts and I prayed over so fervently was impeached for mismanaging state funds.

Leaving

Leaving

"Please make sure your seat belts are securely fastened and place your seat backs and tray tables in the upright position as we prepare to land at Los Angeles International Airport." It was July 1971. As I looked out my window, all I could see through the smog were highways, cars, and houses. As the plane began to sink into that uninviting place, my heart sank also. What an interesting metaphor! After flying high for so many years in Oklahoma, now I had been assigned to a Hispanic parish in East LA, Our Lady of Lourdes. Though I didn't know much Spanish, I had been convincing myself that this would be good for me. Nothing is like immersion to learn another language. Besides, I was being obedient to Abbot Robert, who had sent me. He knew that I liked working with people, gave decent sermons, and was trained in counseling. Maybe here I would find a way to use my skills. All rationalizing aside, I knew why I was sent from Shawnee Oklahoma to LA. It was one of those "in order to avoid scandal" moves.

No one, other than my lover, talked to me about my thoughts or needs, nor did I express them. We, as a community, were losing many members during the turmoil of the '60s. I was one of the few of my age (late 30s) who had remained. There was no forum to help me or others sift through these times, I had eaten of the apple, so I was sent to East LA.

Father Matthew was the pastor of Our Lady of Lourdes. He, a kind and understanding man, had no idea what assignments to give me in the parish other than those he was given when he was an assistant. So I said Mass and gave homilies to people who mostly did not understand what I was saying. I spent many hours sitting in my room in the rectory feeling depressed and lonely. Sometimes I was on call for emergencies. These provided some much needed excitement when I had to rush to a home and anoint a person who was dying or had already died. Another assignment given me by Father Matthew was to collect money at a parish dance. I knew that bingo was not far behind!

What Might Have Happened

George Monk sits in a small room at the rectory of Our Lady of Lourdes, East Los Angeles, California. He is feeling abandoned, lonely, and depressed. George, an old and seasoned therapist from the future, 2008, joins him in his room. It is August, 1971.

GT=George Therapist GM= George Monk
GT "Hi, George. What would you like from me?"
GM "I need to talk about what is going on inside me. I feel depressed, and I know that I am not going to be happy here. I've only been at the parish for a few weeks and have already contacted Bob and Mary Goulding at the Western Institute for Group and Family Therapy. Knowing that they believe I am a good therapist and trainer, I asked them if they had a spot for me on their staff. I studied with them in the Monterey Bay area during the summer of 1970 and for an intensive month this year, 1971. They invited me to come and talk about a way to make it work, and I am happy about that, but still depressed."
GT " It makes sense for you to feel what you feel since you are making a radical change in your life. Have you talked to anyone about all this?"
GM "No, I didn't. Leaving Shawnee and coming here happened so fast. I got a letter from the Abbot giving me the LA assignment while I was at the Institute in June. Maybe I saw it as a way to extricate myself from my lover, or I thought, by being in the parish, I could sort out what I want to do. I am confused and want to

make sense of what's happening to me. Father Amandus, my moral theology and canon law teacher when I was in the seminary, did visit with me at the parish, but only tried to convince me, in leaving the monastery, not to give up my active priesthood. For me, both have been intimately connected. No one in the monastery had reached out to me, nor did I seek any counsel. Leaving wasn't an issue that I dealt with in my own therapy while I was training with Bob and Mary Goulding."

GT "Why was that?"

GM "I got by without working on staying a monk or leaving. I didn't bring it up, but worked on other issues. I guess the "leaving issue" was too threatening. I didn't want to leave; I loved monastic life! At the same time, I was making myself available for relationship with Ruth, a social worker, who was with me during the June workshop this summer. Now I've been intimate with two women. Life has become very complex and being here isn't a solution."

GT "You mentioned earlier that leaving Shawnee and coming here happened so fast. It sounds to me that you have been in the fast lane for quite awhile. When did it begin?"

GM "The Vatican Council II, 1962-65, radically changed monastic life, just as it changed the focus of the over-all church. At St. Gregory's, we were asking our-selves who were we in the modern world. While we were doing this self-study in monastic life, we were also doing it as a requirement for our newly formed coeducational college. In order to obtain North Central accreditation as a college, we had to answer sim-ilar questions as to our mission. During 1962 and 1963 I was attending Oklahoma University for a MBA degree. I was to be the business manager for the college and also for the monastery. Though I followed some of the business track like accounting, business law, and personnel management, I leaned more in the direction of economics and social theory. In order to make it more relevant to me, I researched and wrote my master's thesis on "The Economy of Sixteenth Century English Benedictine Monasticism." It was mostly about how Henry VIII divided up monastic properties. I also included material from Pope John XXIII's encyclical on economic and social justice. I was continuing to attempt the marriage of secular and religious life."

GT "Were you successful at that?"

GM "I finished my degree in 1963. I remember driving back to Shawnee from Oklahoma University and listening to the radio accounts of the Cuban missile crisis. My business manager years, 1963-69, provided fertile ground for my personal crisis. During these six years we got our accreditation and built college housing and dining facilities. As we grew, we began to lose much of our monastic spirit. Monks were running away with female students, while others were finding sexual relationships outside the monastery and eventually left. Feeling very sad at losing each of my brother monks, I continued to hang on, but found it easier to busy myself with college matters while avoiding prayer and interaction with other monks. Abbot Philip, who had been my father figure since I entered the monastery, resigned his position and Robert became out new Abbot. He had been a pastor and administrator at our school. He didn't trust my new age theology, and I didn't trust the goodness of his heart."

GT "What would you say was your biggest trial during this time?"

GM "My father had been a benefactor of the monks for many years. While he was a successful businessman during the '40s, '50s and early '60s, he donated quite a bit of money and goods to the monastery. When his business failed, he and my uncle accepted the position of running the food service for the college. My dad and mother moved to Shawnee to do this. As business manager, technically, I was his boss! It was impossible for my dad and uncle to carry out their work because there were monks who resented having any outsiders running the kitchen and food service that had previously been the territory of monks. It was very painful for me to see what was happening to my dad and uncle. Finally they both quit, realizing that they were given the job without the support to carry it out. As they quit, many thought that I would also. I did frequently resign my job as business manager, but my resignation was not accepted. I was begged to stay on until another monk was trained to replace me."

GT "Is that when you began to become more active outside the walls of the monastery?"

GM "Yes. Though I had studied mystical and spiritual theology for three summers in Chicago and pastoral psychiatry in Ottawa, I wanted more. In the latter '60s I got into a program called psychiatry for general practitioners through Oklahoma University. There I met two psychiatrists who helped me realize my potential as a healer. Boyd Lester was the director of the program, a man I respected, and he respected me. I planned to have him come and help us monks get back on track by meeting with us and doing some group therapy. The monks were not interested or were afraid. The other psychiatrist in the program, Jim Allen, who had worked in the Haight Asbury drug program, helped me establish a center for young people on drugs in Shawnee. A psychologist, Gene Kerfoot, became my friend. He and I came to California in 1970 to train with the Gouldings. After that summer, I continued my relationship with my lover."

GT "Tell me more about her"

GM "She became a friend of my parents, who continued to live in Shawnee. I felt that they were supportive of me having a relationship with her. Noticing that other monks were leaving monasticism, my parents wanted to be part of my journey. As business manager, I was able to borrow a car from a business advisor who owned a dealership, and drove it to California, using it during the summer of 1970 when I was with the Gouldings. At the end of the summer, my lover flew to California with my parents. The four of us drove back to Oklahoma. I think it was our attempt to normalize our relationship, which we continued until my adventures were reported to Abbot Robert later in 1971."

GT "Many factors have contributed to where you are now. I understand more fully the context of your crisis. You are grieving your losses and are fragmented, and it will take a long time to recover your wholeness. You will always be a wounded healer. Sometimes it is easier to say good-bye to what was and what was not, and it is most difficult to say good-bye to what might have been. I will be available to you any time you wish to talk with me."

GM "Thanks, I feel better. It helps to tell my story."

What Did Happen

After only a few weeks, I realized I could not continue in the parish. Before I was assigned to LA, I had spent June training in psychotherapy with Bob and Mary Goulding, who had an institute in Santa Cruz County, California. I had also trained with them the complete previous summer of 1970. I knew they liked my work, so I called them, said I was leaving the parish, and asked if they had a place for me on their staff. Fortunately they did. I told them 1 would be there soon. During this time, Ruth, a social worker who had been in the month-long workshop, was in LA looking for a job. I had fallen in love with her (I was learning how to do this). She also decided to go to Santa Cruz, thinking that she might find work as a social worker at an agency there. We decided to leave together after my Mass on Sunday.

Abbot Robert flew to LA to talk to me before I left. He, after learning my decision, gave me $300. I accepted the money, thinking this was quite a pittance after 20 years of service. Ruth, dressed in orange hot pants, arrived that morning driving her Plymouth named Annie. I was loading her car with my baggage as the Abbot and Father Matthew walked out of the rectory to see me off. I stood in the middle. Not knowing any other words at the time, with the Abbot and my past on one side and Ruth in hot pants and my future on the other, I said, "Father Abbot, I want you to meet my social worker." We climbed into Annie, and I was on my way to a new life.

The Bridge

(Adapted from *Passage (2004-2005 Lecture Notes)* by T. J. Balistrieri, Ed.D)
Printed with Balistieri's permission

You are a person who has given much thought to what you want from life. You have experienced many moods and trials. You have experimented with different ways of living and have had your share of success and failure. At last you begin to see clearly where you want to go.

Diligently, you proceed to find the right opportunity. Sometimes you come close, only to be pushed away. Often you apply all your strength and imagination, only to find the path hopelessly blocked. And then at last it comes. But the opportunity will not wait. It has been made available only for a short time. If it were seen that you are not committed, the opportunity will not come again.

Eager to arrive, you start on your journey. With each step, you want to move faster, with each thought about your goal, your heart beats quicker, with each vision of what lies ahead, you find renewed vigor. Strength that has left you returns, and all kinds of dormant desires reawaken within you.

Hurrying along, you come upon a bridge built high above a river in order to protect it from the floods of spring. You start across. Then you notice someone coming from the opposite direction. As the person draws closer, it seems as though the person is coming to greet you. You can see clearly, however, that you do not know this person who is dressed similarly except for something tied around the person's waist.

When you are within hailing distance, you can see that what is about the person's waist is a rope. It is wrapped several times, and probably, if extended would reach a length of 30 feet.

Just as you are noticing this fact, the other begins to uncurl the rope, and as you are coming closer, the other says, " Pardon me, would you be so kind as to hold the end a moment? "

Surprised by this request, which is made so politely, you agree without a thought, reach out and take it.

"Thank you" says the other, then adds, "two hands now, and remember, hold tight." At that point the other jumps off the bridge.

Within a second the free falling body hurtles the distance of the rope's length and from the bridge you instantly feel the pull. Instinctively you hold tight. The weight almost drags you off the bridge. You manage to brace yourself against the edge, however, and after having caught your breath, you look down at the other dangling distantly close to oblivion.

"What are you trying to do?" you yell.

"Just hold tight," says the other.

"This is ridiculous" you think, and begin trying to haul the other in. You cannot get the leverage. It is as though the weight of the other person and the length of the rope have been carefully calculated in advance so that together they create a counter weight just beyond your strength to bring the other back to safety. "Why did you do this?" you call out.

"Remember," says the other, "if you let go, I will be lost."

"I am your responsibility," says the other.

"Well, I did not ask for it," you say.

"If you let go, I am lost," repeats the other.

You begin to look around for help. But there is no one. How long would you have to wait? Why did this happen to you now just as you are on the verge of true success? You examine the side, searching for a place to tie the rope. Maybe there is some protrusion, perhaps, or maybe a hole in the boards. There is no way to get rid of this new -found burden, even temporarily.

"What do you want?" you ask the other hanging below.

"Just your help," the other answers.

"How can I help I cannot pull you in and there is no place to tie the rope so I can go and find someone to help me help you. "

"I know that," says the other. "Just hang on. That will be enough. Tie the rope around your waist, it will be easier."

Fearing that your arms can't hold out much longer, you tie the rope around your waist.

"Why did you do this?" you repeat. "Don't you see what you have done? What possible purpose could you have in mind?"

"Just remember," says the other. My life is in your hands."

What should you do? If you let go, all your life you will know that you let the other die. If you stay you risk losing your momentum towards your own long sought after salvation. Either way this will haunt you forever. With ironic humor you think to die yourself, instantly, to jump off the bridge while still holding on. You think, "That would teach this fool." But you want to live and to live life fully. What a choice you have to make. How shall you ever decide?

Soon time goes by, but sill no one comes. The critical moment of decision is drawing near. To show your commitment to your own goals, you would have to continue on your journey now. It is already almost too late to arrive in time. What a terrible choice to have to make.

A new thought occurs to you. While you cannot pull the other up by your own efforts alone, if the other could shorten the rope from the other's end by curling it around the person's waist, together you could do it. Actually the other could do it alone, as long as you do, standing on the bridge, keeps it still and steady.

"Now listen, you shout down. I think I know how to save you." You explain your plan, but the other isn't interested.

"You mean you won't help? But I told you I cannot pull you up myself, and I don't think I can hang on much longer either."

"You must try," the other shouts back in tears. "I you fail, I die."

The point of decision has arrived. What should you do? What an impossible decision to have to make: your life or the other's. And then, you have an idea, a really new idea! It is so new, in fact, it almost borders on revelation, and so foreign it is to your traditional way of thinking.

"I want you to listen carefully because I mean what I am about to say. I will not accept the position of choice for your life, only for my own. The choice for your life, I give back to you."

"What do you mean?" the other asks, afraid.

"I mean, simply, it's up to you.. You decide which way this ends. I will become the counter weight. You do the pulling and bring yourself up. I will even tug a little from here." You begin unwinding the rope from around your waist and brace yourself anew against the side.

"You cannot mean what you say," the other shrieks. "YOU WOULD NOT BE SO SELFISH. I AM YOUR RESPONSIBILITY. What could be so important that you would let someone die? Do not do this to me. You wait a moment. There is no change in the tension of the rope. "I accept your choice," you say at last, and free you hands.

Earthy Living –
George Dismounts from His Horse

Abbot Robert's Letter of December 15, 1971:
Saint Gregory's Abbey
Shawnee, Oklahoma 74801
Office of the Abbot
Rev. George McClendon O.S.B.
Dear Father George:

I received your letter on Monday. I have written to Fr. Maxell giving him the information you requested. I had had a letter from him, also.

Word of your desire to laicize was not unexpected. The only aspect of the matter that concerns me is the obvious compulsiveness of it all. After all, only last May you were insisting you wanted to remain a priest and a monk. In July you accepted a parish assignment ostensibly to avoid a situation in Shawnee. A few weeks later you wanted a leave. And now the works. I think you need psychiatrist.

Once you have gotten the necessary dispensations, I sure hope you will not enter a marriage with such compulsion. You ought to know it could only spell disaster for you and some poor girl.

I wish you God's blessings and good fortune in your work and in the years that are ahead of you.
Sincerely in Christ Jesus,
Robert G. Dodson, O.S.B

Ruth definitely was not some "poor girl." She and I would lie on the living room floor of Bob and Mary's house, a room in which many therapists made redecisions about their lives during the month-long workshop of June, 1971. Lying there, Ruth and I listened to the song from *Jesus Christ*

Superstar, "I Don't Know how to Love Him." Sung by Mary Magdalene, it was prophetic in our relationship: *"I don't know how to love him. What to do, how to move him... He's a man. He's just a man...I never thought I'd come to this. What's it all about?"* I did not see myself as Jesus Christ, nor had I accepted myself as a man, just a man. Who was I, really?

After I left monasticism, Ruth became my Lady Dragon companion for six years, 1971-1976. She and I privately vowed to be with each other as wife and husband. I am forever honored that she took McClendon as her private and professional name and kept it after we were no longer together. We were quite fortunate and successful as associates of Bob and Mary Goulding at the Western Institute For Group and Family Therapy in Watsonville, California. We became the "Family Therapy" side of the institute.

One day while Ruth and I were renting a house in Watsonville, we decided to visit a private and expensive conclave of seaside homes called Pajaro Dunes. We pretended that we were looking to buy a condominium and thereby got inside the gate. During our tour we came upon a house for sale. We both dreamed how wonderful such a place would be to live in while doing training and our practice. Of course we could not afford it, since I had not made any income for over 20 years. Shortly after we saw the house, I received a phone call from the developer of the place who suggested that he buy the home, and Ruth and I buy it back from him. I later found out that he discovered my background and he, maybe a "guilty" Catholic, wanted to help.

The house was to become the beach location for the Western Institute For Group and Family Therapy, and it was there that we lived and worked and became financially successful. It was a place where we listened to families and individuals, teaching them to foster changes in their lives. We ran workshops at home and traveled extensively to train mental health professionals and have them view us working with families. Ruth had more experience in this than I, and she also had a greater dedication than I to develop and expand our work. I remember joking with her after we had scheduled yet another workshop after having just completed one: "Why don't we schedule one and then cancel it?"

It wasn't that I was burned out from so much work and travel; I simply became less and less available. I was depressed, drank and ate too much, and felt I was working too much. I eventually did my own therapy (at Ruth's suggestion) and discovered that I was passively going along with her program and was expressing my anger by shutting down to her in our work and in our relationship.

I was out of balance because I had not integrated the monastic side of myself with the professional side. It seemed that the more we advanced our work, the more I withdrew into myself. I had not grieved my loss. I don't blame Ruth for my unfinished work. She loved me, and I loved her. Maybe we simply went as far as we could together. Our breakup in 1977 was painful, but our directions became different. Though Ruth and I rarely meet anymore, we still love each other and are grateful for our shared journey.

A year later, Carol and I started dating. While Ruth and I were together, I had applied to Rome for dispensation from my monastic and priestly vows. Twice I was denied a dispensation. After meeting Carol, I applied a third time to Pope Paul VI.

August 19, 1977

Most Holy Father,

I am writing to request release from my monastic and priestly vows. It is my purpose in this letter to give my reasons for making such a request. This is a renewal of my former requests, which were denied in 1971 and 1972.

I have not been practicing as a priest or monk since August of 1971 and have no intention of doing so in the future. I believe that during these six years I have given this important matter much prayerful thought and still maintain my resolve to obtain my release.

Currently, I am actively involved with my work as a successful teacher, counselor and psychotherapist. Also, I have been attending mass at my local parish wherein, with the exception of the pastor, I am not known as a priest or monk.

It is my firm desire to remain active in the church sharing my expertise with the parish community and eventually marrying in the church.

Therefore, I again request release from my vows in order that I might in good conscience continue to practice my faith and help others to do so.

George H. McClendon

To my joy and surprise I received a Latin document from Rome, dated December 10, 1977, giving me my dispensations.

SACRA CONGREGATIO
PRO DOCTRINA FIDEI
Prot. N. 527/72s.

Reverndissime Domine,

Dnus GEORGE HAROLD McCLENDON, secerdos professus Congregationis Helveto-Americanae O.S.B.

Petiit reductionem ad statum laicalem cum dispensatione ab omnibus oneribus e sacris Ordinibus (et a religiosa Professione) manantibus, non excepto onere servandi legem sacri coelibatus.

S.S. D. N. PAULUS, Divina Providentia Papa VI, die 10 Decembris,1977, habita relatione de case a Sacra Congretione pro Doctrina Fidei, adnuere dignatus est pro gratia juxta sequentes Normas:

He seeks a reduction to the lay state with dispensation from all obligations of holy Orders and from the vows of religious Profession, not excluding the obligation of keeping the law of holy celibacy.

Most Holy Father Paul, by Divine Providence Pope VI, on the tenth day of December, 1977, with the case having been given to the Sacred Congregation of the Doctrine of Faith, deigned it worthy according to the following Norms:

In summary, these norms required that I could not choose to receive the dispensation and continue to function as a priest except in extreme circumstances. Also, if I were to marry, I should have the ceremony in a place where I was not known as a priest and the wedding be as private as possible. I should not, where I am known to be a priest, ever have a part in liturgical celebrations. I should not give homilies. I should not have any pastoral office or be in charge of a seminary or be a spiritual director there. Nor should I teach in a seminary or be on a theological faculty. I should not teach religion in schools where there would be a fear of scandal or "admiration."

In April of 1996, a reporter from the *Monterey Peninsula Herald* interviewed me for an article about my journey. I explained that church law allowed me to function as a priest in "extremis," meaning in extreme circumstances. She asked me if I find any such circumstances. I replied, "All the time."

Carol and I were married on June 17, 1978. Father Joe Watt, a dear friend, was the priest at our wedding. The wedding took place under the redwood trees on land which Carol and I bought to build our home. On May 25, 1979, she gave birth to our (Gemini) twin daughters: Sarah and Jennifer. After all those years surrounded by men, I now was blessed with a feminine community. Mary Goulding, upon hearing that news, said "George, now you are a *real* father!"

Wedding

baby daughters

toddlers

Path to Synthesis – What I Have Learned and Taught Along the Way

What Do You Say After You Say Good-bye?

Eric Berne, the founder of transactional analysis, in 1970 wrote a book entitled, *What Do You Say After You Say Hello?* I considered entitling this book, *What Do You Say After You Say good-bye?*

Although I made a decision in August of 1971 to leave monastic life and the practice of my priesthood, I have been in the process of writing a new autonomous life story since that time.

Who Are You Really? Who Is George? Who Is Dragon?

Ever since that woman asked me "who are you really?", I have been seeking the answer. Who am I? I believe that is the basic spiritual question. It is also the basic spiritual-relational question: "Who are we, really?" Today, we are similarly confronted with this important question as many of our familiar structures are in trouble. Who is the corporation, really: the CEOs, the stockholders, employees? Who is the Church really: the hierarchy, the priest, laity? Who is America really? Who are we? What do we want?

I have been a therapist to many couples over my 30 years of practice. I have constantly seen them coming to sessions protecting themselves or wanting to prove the other wrong. The marital structure is fragmented, and they are in survival. The danger is that they have forgotten who they are and are acting as caricatures of themselves. One of the most useful interventions I have is to simply introduce them. "John, this is Mary. Mary, this is John." Once they remember who they are, it is a lot easier to deal with the issues. This remembering is crucial as a first step. I have known couples that have solved their problems and lost their relationships. Being who they are must be far more important than the problems.

Years ago I saw a film called The Full Monty. *It depicted what happened to men who had worked in the steel mill in Sheffield England after the mill closed down. Losing employment left them in survival mode and affected their lives dramatically. Gary could not pay child support to his ex wife. Dave was not able to perform sexually because of his low self-esteem. Gerald lied to his wife and pretended to go to work every day for six months. Another man attempted suicide. They all tried various ways to solve their problems and were not successful. Then they found a way. Gary, after seeing the interest the women in Sheffield had for male dancers, Chippendale dancers, and seeing how much money these men earned, convinced the unemployed men to do their own dance show. This very funny movie shows their awkwardness as they risk doing the dance. They had to move together in order to make it work. It took the dance, Yorkshire style to connect them with themselves and ultimately the women in their lives. In one moving scene, Jean, Dave's wife who suffered the loss of his sexual attention, encouraged him to dance.*

Becoming male strippers and appearing full monty provides the connection. Each man had to strip himself of much: Gary, being the loser, Dave of his self-contempt, Gerald his lie and one man his suicide solution, another his age and another his inability to dance up the wall like Donald O'Connor. It is in the stripping of these definitions, these habits, and appearing full monty that these men became whole. They appear naked, and in this nakedness, being just who they are, they are quite enough. And so are we.

Unmasked

Not long ago I saw two other films that address an important issue in our society where looking good, selling self, and being acceptable by one's peers are so important. Especially in an election year, candidates must appear to be electable. Each is marketed to convince us that he or she will be our hero, saving us from terrorists or unemployment. They put on the masks and say the words their handlers determine the electorate wants to hear. The two films, Spiderman II *and* Open Range *present scenarios where the hero unmasks himself and risks acceptance or rejection based simply on being who he is.*

Peter Parker, unmasked Spiderman, finally lets Mary Jane see who he is and what he feels. She had kissed Spider-

man, but never had kissed Peter Parker. Peter, knowing he must always be fighting crime and be on call for emergencies, did not want to burden Mary Jane with Spiderman's mission. Peter and we viewers are relieved to learn that he can be Spiderman and Peter Parker, sacrificing neither, and still be loved. In a crucial scene on a runaway train while fighting another of his nemeses, he has his mask ripped from his face. A little boy seeing Spiderman unwillingly reveal his true identity says, "Don't worry, Spiderman, we won't tell anyone." His identity was safe with the children. Maybe we can risk believing that our relationships can handle our true identity.

Open Range *is a film starring Kevin Costner as Charlie Waite and Robert Duval as Boss Spearman. They come into a typical western town to kill the bad guys who killed one of their own men and are persecuting the good people of the community. Boss and Charlie's task is clear and they both know they too might be gunned down. Boss says, "It's a good day to die." The plot gets complicated because Charlie falls in love with Sue, who is the sister of the local doctor.*

Once again the hero has fallen in love while following his mission. "A man has to do what a man must do." Once the heart of the hero is wounded with cupid's arrow, he is faced with a terrible dilemma. In an Atlantic Monthly *article entitled "What if John Wayne Didn't Ride Out of Town" What if he did not say, "I've got to be movin' on, Ma'am."?*

Charlie Waite does ride out of town after all the killing is over. Sue tells him she will not wait forever. He considers this and returns to the woman he loves. He tells her that she should not love him since he is a killer, but she and we know who he really is.

Who are we under our masks? It is risky to remove our facades that we present to the world. We decided long ago that it was not safe to be who we really are, to feel what we feel, and to express our feelings and ourselves publicly.

Let's revisit our original decisions and decide again if being ourselves is enough to perform adequately, enough to be believable, enough to be lovable.

If we decide to take the risk, we must go all the way. The army advertisement states: "Be all you can be, join the Army." We have held back being all that we can be. If we don't do it now, when will we? If I am not an authority now, when will I be? Being all that we are is necessary for creativity. We restrict ourselves in survival; we express ourselves in creativity.

What are the North, South, East and West of me? The four directions, so sacred to ancient peoples, can serve as a template for wholeness. The North of me is my Priesthood. The South of me is my Monastic tradition. The East of me is my Cherokee heritage. The West of me is my calling to be a Healer. I must integrate all these directions to be who I am, really. Who are you?

One summer I sat with about 20 people, men and women, in a sweat lodge. We were doctors, nurses, therapists, and teachers. Before we entered the darkness of the lodge, each of us dealt with anxiety in our own ways. Some joked, some told stories, some sat in silence. Finally we crawled through the open flap covering the tent-like space within. We sat in a circle, thigh to thigh, as our Indian elder began the ceremony.

For two and a half hours we sat on the ground in the dark sweating as red-hot rocks were placed into the center of our space. We prayed together, we sang, we told stories, and we perspired together. Our masks melted away, as did our mascara and deodorants. We were wet together in a womb. At the end we crawled out into the light as if re-birthed. Soaked, we hugged each other, said our good-byes. We went our separate directions seeking to reunite with our supportive communities to live our lives unmasked.

Who Shows Up?
Will Dragon Leave the Darkness for Her Light?
Will George Embrace His Darkness?

You have examined the three monastic vows support-
ing the Benedictine way of spiritual practice: Stability (being
in sacred and ordinary space), Obedience (thorough listen-
ing, consciousness), and Conversation Morum (conversion,
change). The following chapters describe how to get ready
for the spiritual journey.

The space between what you know and what is possi-
ble is full of mystery and life yet to be lived. The familiar, pre-
dictable, safe, and painful way has provided a form of
security on which you have relied. It is difficult to launch into
the mystery because it is unknown, surprising, and risky.
Because you know it well, you hold on, protecting yourself in
pain.

I ask a client, "Who are you?"

"This is who I am."

"Yes, but who are you really?"

"I don't know, but I know who I want to be."

"Then be it."

"That is too frightening."

"Why?"

"If I let myself be who I want to be, I will be rejected
or criticized."

"So?"

"I don't want either of those."

"That is what you don't want. What do you want?"

"I want to be who I want to be."

"Then be it."

"That is too frightening."

I frequently ask people, "How do you get ready for what you want? How do you get ready to be satisfied? How do you get ready to make love or to enjoy a good meal, music, or a sunset?" I receive a puzzled look, and am told that they don't know. They have forgotten how. I am pleased when my clients have a child under the age of five in their family. She still remembers, even if they don't. A child can be our teacher! At that age, in most cases, she is not defined by fear. She is hopeful, trusting and full of wonder. Not getting what she wants, she may cry and have a tantrum. Following that ritual, in loving families, she returns to the "want pursuit" with outstretched arms.

You have become an expert at scarcity and FPSP (Familiar, Predictable, Safe, and Painful) living, you have collected enough evidence of rejection, disappointment and even abandonment, to justify not taking risks. The recovery process may be a difficult. First, you need to be a loving parent to yourself and receive support from those who love you while building a tolerance for abundance. Before becoming proficient, at first, you may not know what to do with it. Have you ever watched a baby who is overstimulated? Sometimes all the child can do is cry. Sometimes a young child will spill the milk or break something. Sometimes a budding adolescent will do something equally disturbing when, though the teenager has developed into the body of an adult, sometimes he/she still behaves like a child. You also need room to not know what to do when faced with the rush of fullness. I have found it helpful to encourage grown men and women to give themselves new parenting with permission, protection, and potency. They need some slack until they can grow into abundance. Loving, caring, accepting partners can create a place of safety where they can listen and not move beyond supportive structures that make assimilation possible. This is a place of abundance.

You receive training in getting ready for something bad to happen. The insurance industry would not thrive as well in our society if you did not accept your need for protection from catastrophe. Sometimes you take small risks in policies by carrying a deductible.

When you and I were young children, maybe three or four years old, we naturally got ready for something good to happen to us. The child with outstretched arms, the child expecting to be loved and protected, is available for what will come.

A father told me about his little boy who excitedly told him that the boy's mother was going to have a party for him when they arrived home. The father tried to convince the child that this was not the case. The boy would not give up his joyful expectation. When they arrived home, there was no party. The boy felt disappointed, but was soon off on a new positive expectation.

Acting "As If"

Before I became a monk, I spent time, especially in my year as a novice, acting "as if" I were a monk.

You may remember Oral Roberts, the evangelist from Oklahoma. In a very spirit-filled manner, he would proclaim to his radio listeners that "something good was going to happen to you." They believed, sent in their donations, and got ready for that eventuality. No doubt, for many, something good did happen. Oral Robert's listeners acted "as if."

Successful sex is a metaphor for this phenomenon. Foreplay is a getting ready for the event. Foreplay itself has a beginning, middle, and end before we move to the event, e.g. intercourse. The anticipation of "something good happening" prepares us for something good to happen. Even if the event doesn't work, we still had the foreplay, and wasn't it fun! When the event is successfull, we are all the more prepared to celebrate! How do you get ready for what you want?

How do you get ready for acceptance, just for being who you truly are?

Acting "as if" is the essential practice for getting ready. You begin to fantasize, practicing optimism, scheduling a time and place for the event. Physiology is affected by this getting ready. You salivate when you get ready for a meal, are sexually aroused when ready to make love, experience a longing for what you want or the person you want. These forces help in approaching the object of your desire with confidence.

Acting "as if" is very different from pretending. A pretender does not believe that he has what it takes. Acting "as if" includes knowledge of ability. Before an expert or an accomplished actor or athlete performs, he or she must first act as if he or she can do it. Many visualize themselves being successful before a performance. After collecting enough evidence, it becomes much easier to act accomplished. Accepting yourself (your wholeness) helps you know you have what it takes.

Some people tell me that they are afraid that they will lose what they have accomplished; whether this be health goals attained after years of illness and being overweight, sobriety attained after years of drunkenness, or a relationship that finally satisfies the person's desires. It is as if it is not safe for fulfillment of one's desires. I sometimes ask what my wife, Carol, has asked me many times. The question is simply, "Is it all right for you?" When I ask that question, I often get the reply that of course it is OK. Then I prepare myself to hear from them the magic word, "But." Every word following that disjunctive adverb speaks to the danger of trusting too much, the danger of becoming complacent or secure. Here are some examples of the rapid movement from the left side of the "but" to the right side:

LEFT SIDE	RIGHT SIDE
"I really feel good when she says that she loves me	BUT she only tells me when I ask her."
"He hasn't had a drink for six months	BUT he will get drunk again with his friends
"I trust my daughter	BUT she's irresponsible with money."
"That was a great meal you prepared	BUT I would have cooked the fish differently."
"We have wonderful sex	BUT not often enough."
"I know you love me	BUT if you only knew....
"I want to be an athlete	BUT I'll never make it."

Perhaps these might remind you of other examples.

Even after a person has recovered from addiction abuse or a series of failed relationships, she or he must still build a tolerance for health. Health is a word that comes from hale as in "hale and hardy." Hale derives from the same root word as wholeness or holiness. You must first be hale before we can be holy. You learned to survive in the face of shortages of love, affection, safety, and respect. Evidence of these shortages, or predicted shortages, shows up on the right side of the "but."

Abundance is related to creativity and not survival. Howard Frankl, a therapist and friend of mine, suggests that the left side of the but is controlled by the right side, or creative side, of the brain, and the right side of the but is controlled by the left side of the brain, the logical or evidence-gathering side.

I encourage clients to dream or fantasize that something good is going to happen. I encourage them to "act as if" they will get what they do want.

Opening up the possibility of fulfillment increases the creative juices that lie inside of you, making more of you available to the more outside. You may not deserve the love and caring that someone bestows on you because of your past and all the bad things you have done. It is no wonder that it is so difficult to accept being accepted.

A client of mine, who was mugged in New York City, told me, "Thank God it happened to someone like me."

I reminded him of Groucho Marx's comment, "I wouldn't join a club that would accept someone like me."

In religion, calling oneself a sinner is the beginning of conversion, so also with the survival self. Declaring oneself wounded by incest, abuse, codependency, and incapable of lasting relationships, is the beginning of change. The next step is to be open to grace, love freely given, bestowed on us by God, our friends, and lovers. Our practice demands that we be humble in the face of such abundance, be grateful for the gift, and hopefully learn how to give the gift to ourselves. All this takes place on the left side of the "but."

A Place Where We Can Be Who We Are: Wholeness and Fragmentation

Since the mission of George is to
Slay the dragon, he must
experience her as Other.
She, fearing death, protects herself,
and only ventures from her dark place
while breathing fire.

David Bohm, famous quantum physicist and philosopher, in his book *Wholeness and The Implicate Order*, declares that…."wholeness is what is real…what is needed is …to give attention to {the} habit of fragmentary thought, to be aware of it, and thus bring it to an end. Man's approach to reality may then be whole, and so the response will be whole… it is crucial {to} be aware of the activity of …thought as such; i.e. as a form of insight; a way of looking, rather than as a true copy of reality as it is."

If "wholeness is what is real," then your worldview may not lead to wholeness (holiness or haleness). Maybe the true "original" sin is settling for the fragments when you are, as a human being, truly whole. If your story is about fear, fight, or flight, you do your best to defend against what you do not want, aligning yourself with others who are doing the same, assenting to a particular view of holiness, for example, encouraging one another to avoid the evil that lurks just outside a shared place of safety. Sometimes these communities are families, churches, even nations. Some have been "saved," while others are "lost." The task of the "saved" is to evangelize the others so that they, too, can avoid hell and damnation. "I'm OK – you're not OK." This is, of course, another fragmentation.

From this worldview we build structures, pass laws, and elect leaders to further a specific way of viewing reality. We even go to war and lay down our lives in the name of such a view. When defined by this way if thinking, you and I learn about survival and forget individual creativity. You may live in a very small frame and believe it to be the universe. It becomes familiar because it is closely tied to your family survival tactics. "The way to survive (avoid rejection and abandonment) in this family is not to ————-" is predictable because you know what will happen. The formula is "If I ....you will ... ... instead of ....therefore I........." is safe because you do not have to take risks and are safe from what you do not want is painful, but it a pain you know well. When you and I were children, we would say to ourselves, as we skipped down the sidewalk, "Don't step on a crack or you will break your mother's back." Inevitably, no matter how carefully we navigated, we would step on a crack.

You may have entered a relationship in an attempt to avoid loneliness. The thinking is, "If I am with this person, I will never feel lonely, rejected, or abandoned again." Notice this is what the person does not want. We call these relationships "codependent." They do not necessarily help us obtain what we do want. Just as we ultimately step on the crack, or sin, so also in these relationships we will eventually experience loneliness, rejection, and abandonment.

One of my favorite photographs is that of a young child running to the ocean with her arms outstretched as if to embrace the sea and all of creation: "Hello world!" Originally, you are blessed. Knowing about unity, wholeness, and holiness, you had to learn to forget. This is the original sin, the sin of the human condition leading to fragmentation. Catholic theology has changed its definition of "original" sin:

"Recent formulations underscore the tendency to view original sin in terms of the concrete situation of human life and society rather than as a taint transmitted biologically through human history. The doctrine of original sin is thus expressed in contemporary Catholic thought less as a 'catechism truth' valorizing infant baptism and more as a useful category for the analysis of the tragic human condition" (*Encyclopedia of Catholicism*, p. 944).

The Greek word for sin translates "to miss the mark." The little child resonating to the ocean still remembers. She is right on the mark. Maybe this is what Jesus meant when he told us to become like little children. Between birth and death, you are on a journey from wholeness to fragmentation, and hopefully, returning to wholeness. The young girl who opens her arms to abundance, life in its wholeness, learns to close her body, her heart, and her soul. She learns not to take risks, and she lives as if there is a shortage instead of an abundance. She avoids what she does not want to happen. She fears the loss of security. She becomes compliant to avoid rejection or abandonment.

One fear we all share is the fear of death. It is an unknown; it is an ending of life as we know it. The term "rigor mortis" refers to the rigidity of the body after death.

My daughter, Sarah, at the age of four or five, came to her mother and me announcing that, "Hermie (her pet hermit crab) is dead." I asked how she knew. She replied, "When I pick him up in his shell and turn him over, he falls out." He was dead!

Sometimes we opt for a rigidity of life, a "rigor vitae," which is familiar, predictable, safe, and painful. This is a pain we know and share with others.

My wife, Carol, had a cartoon attached to the mirror in our bathroom. It depicted a very dark cave. All the viewer could see was a set of eyes peering from the darkness. The caption under the cartoon read, "If you don't take any risks, nothing bad-or good-will happen."

The little girl forgot who she was. Terror over possible loss quenched her creative reaching out to abundance. My hope for her as well as for us is that we begin to experiment with opening up ourselves again to wholeness, to take the risk of being who we truly are.

Spirituality as Relationship: Will George and Dragon Lady Listen to Their Inner Soundings and Discover a Shared Harmony?

A workshop led by my friends, Khalila and Richard, gave clear clues to the meaning of spirituality. The title of the day was "Finding Your Voice." First we practiced silence, breathing, and listening. I was particularly moved by the exercise in which we listened to a single note that Richard played on the piano. Since the workshop took place in my home, being extra conscious of noise, I worried that the refrigerator's whirl coming from the kitchen was a distraction. The note was not lost and somehow found its own place together with the refrigerator.

Khalila strummed a shruti, a many stringed East Indian instrument that means place. Accompanied by her, we made "om" sounds while coming to "our place" inside. We LISTENED. We resonated and reverberated together. We CHANGED or modulated, shaping our mouths while adjusting our vocal cords, breath, and posture. We sang with our own voices in RELATION to one another.

Singing in harmony is a fit metaphor when explaining spirituality as relationship. While I was a Benedictine monk, I lived in a community where, together, we worked, prayed, and sang Gregorian chants. On the day of the workshop, I listened and sounded my "oms" with my friends.

The Benedictine way of spirituality is the middle way. Monks learn to find their place, walk carefully, and balance between stability and change. This path is not about mediocrity. Often a more difficult practice than more radical ones, it requires careful listening, changing one's life, and choosing to be in harmony with others. Leaving community and becoming a hermit in the mountains has its own discipline, but may not be more taxing than living in community, listening to the common drone and to one's own soundings. Community life is a place of consensus, demanding mindfulness of self and others.

　　Outside monastic life we have many opportunities to practice the middle way in our relationships. A client of mine told me that because of a problem with his hip and constant pain, his practice was to accept his condition and be patient with himself. By doing that he was able to be kinder and more present to his family. He was less reactive and more active towards them, showing them more love and acceptance, as he needed both for his own condition.

　　"Love your neighbor as you love yourself." Maybe if we truly "knew" our own condition (Socrates' "Know Thyself") we would better understand and love others.

　　This continues to be the Place-Thoroughly Listen-Change model I have been underlining in my writing. How simple and not easy at all! I pray that I become simpler in my ways. Complexities in my life displace me from me. I lose track of the note I want to hear. I abandon the place of listening and tend to experience the stress of displacement.
Refugee from my center
Displaced by wants, not needs,
I listen no more
To the voice within.

Where have I gone?
Distracted, off track.
Come home, come home
To the place within.

Here, now, listen!
Resonate, reverberate to
Whispering, whispering
Of the spirit within.

Carly Simon, the composer and performer of *You're So Vain*, said in an interview that the reason people believe she is also writing songs about herself is that she taps into the Universal. Songs about someone else are about her, and songs about her are about everyone else. Isn't this the way it is? Our veil from the universe is very thin. Most of the time we live as if we are not connected. Simply allow ourselves to be here now, listen to the "whispering," and simply respond. This is a definition of prayer.

The Map Is Not the Territory

Will George risk letting go of
the hero caricature of himself?
Will Dragon risk letting go of
her fiery defensiveness?

Gregory Bateson, whom I often quote as one of my
mentors, taught me that the "map is not the territory." I count
myself fortunate to have been one of his students and hearing
these words, followed by his infectious laughter. He, using a
Socratic teaching method, would pose questions instead of
imparting information. As an example, he asked, "Why does
a mirror reverse an image from left to right and not from top
to bottom?" He asked us many "Why" questions. Gregory
was a philosopher who wanted us to be philosophers. He
challenged us to have experiences with all kinds of data, not
relying on what someone said about their own findings. He
wanted us to feel the confusion, clarity, wonder, and awe as
we explored the process of first-hand learning. His kind of
scientist was one who takes the risk of direct contact with the
territory. The map is only a statement describing the "territory."

In his book *Deep Survival*, Laurence Gonzales
describes how we misuse our maps when we are lost:
"The research suggests five general stages in the process a
person goes through when lost. In the first, you deny that
you're disoriented and press on with growing urgency,
attempting to make your mental map fit what you see. In the
next stage, as you realize that you're genuinely lost, the
urgency blossoms into a full-scale survival emergency. Clear
thought becomes impossible and action becomes frantic,

unproductive even dangerous. In the third stage (usually following injury or exhaustion), you expend the chemicals of emotion and form a strategy for finding some place that matches the mental map. (It is a misguided strategy for there is no such place now: you are lost.) In the fourth stage, you deteriorate both rationally and emotionally as the strategy fails to resolve the conflict. In the final stage as you run out of options and energy, you must make a new mental map of where you are. You must become Robinson Crusoe or you will die. To survive, you must find your self. Then it won't matter where you are" (pp. 166–167).

This is crisis, the turning point. Will you remember who you are? The Native Americans have a saying: "You are not lost, the trees know where you are." Finding this is crucial at survival and creative, mystical, edges. Who are you, where are you?

I am often asked what the difference is between spirituality and religion. Religion is the map of the spiritual experience. It is not the territory. When entering sacred time and space, you come as a Christian, Jew, Muslim, Hindu, Buddhist, Native American, African, or Atheist. This provides the structure to function in sacred space. It is a filter through which you experience. It is not the experience. Mystics and spiritual seekers of every tradition must let go of that tradition long enough to be immersed into the mystery. Once you, the seeker, returns to an ordinary place, you can use creed or culture to describe your journey. We, as Gonzales states, are lost in uncharted territory. We still attempt to make our belief map fit. Some give up the spiritual journey because it is too threatening to be off the map. Continuing on the journey often requires you to be lost so that you can remember who you are. John of the Cross described this passage as the "Dark Night of the Soul."

Passing through, letting go of your map, you enter into sacred space. There is fear upon entering that is different from survival fear. This fear is not about the scarcity of love, but its abundance. We often have difficulty accepting uncon-ditional love. The great mystics describe their experiences in erotic metaphors. St. Teresa of Avila and John of the Cross speak of it as meeting their lover. The Song of Songs in the Old Testament uses the same description. Poetry is the lan-guage of those who live at the creative, mystical margin.

Dogma and belief informs the experience. Experience reforms the dogma. We come to a place where we can say the same words used by Carl Jung. He was asked if he believed in God. He answered, "I don't believe in God, I know God."

Map and Territory—Part II

In 1970 while I was still a Benedictine monk, I attended a retreat at a monastery in Pecos, New Mexico. The form of spirituality they practiced was charismatic. These were the days when some in the Church were experimenting with prayer based on inspiration from the Holy Spirit. At Pecos, we would pray and sing and speak as the Spirit moved us. Some would speak in tongues, called *glossolalia*. Some would perform spiritual healing. This form of spirituality has a strong biblical base.

In Acts 2:1-5 we read:
"When the day of Pentecost came it found them gathered in one place. Suddenly from up in the sky there came a noise like a strong, driving wind, which was heard, all through the house where they were seated. Tongues as of fire appeared which parted and came to rest on each of them. All were filled with the Holy Spirit. They began to express themselves in foreign tongues and make bold proclamation as the Spirit prompted them."

When I returned to my monastery, I found ways to use more spontaneous prayer in my work as chaplain at our college. I am sure I was full of enthusiasm as I spoke about my experience of God. Also I am certain that I was a problem for Abbot Robert, the head of our monastery. He tended to be conservative and somewhat untrusting of the new "religious freedom." He called me into his office and asked me an important question, which I did not adequately answer at the time. His question was, "What does all this have to do with theology or religion?"

Thirty-four years later I write this piece as, at least, a partial answer to his question.

Religion

All religions are based on teachings usually contained in sacred documents such as the Bible or the Koran. In addition to these, there is also a tradition that helps the believers support their convictions. A tradition is formed by continuous beliefs held by the followers throughout an extended period of history. Sometimes tradition may have as much to say about a religious belief as the sacred documents. These two sources combine to create a theology.

A dogma proclaims what must be believed, and a moral code spells out the conduct requirements to be followed. Often there are church laws that are an addition to divine laws. The church laws may or may not carry the same weight as the divine.

Religions have some form of hierarchy. These leaders minister either directly to the believing communities or sit in control positions to maintain the integrity of belief and conduct.

Religions have rituals, sacraments, and various prayer and worship forms that support believers in their lives on the spiritual path. Many see their religion as a way to reach heaven. They may be called the "saved." Some religions emphasis sin, forgiveness, and the importance of sanctifying grace.

Though this is by no means an exhaustive description, I want to establish how important the structure of belief and organization is to maintain the integrity of any religion.

Spirituality

When I was a novice monk, eager to move ahead on my spiritual path, I had to learn about structure. My novice master forbade me to read anything written by Thomas Merton, a modern mystic, until I learned how to be a stable monk.

I was required to study the rule of St. Benedict, the Scriptures and a little book called the *Tyrocenium*. This was a book containing all the rules for being an obedient and humble monk. Only after I had learned some basics of monasticism and theology was I allowed to read Merton and other spiritual writers such as John of the Cross or Teresa of Avila. We had not yet been exposed to Buddhist spirituality, though Merton was working at bridging Eastern and Western monastic traditions. It was difficult for me to be patient and wait until I was seasoned enough to absorb his writings.

In spiritual practice we all tend to pass through three stages. The first stage is the <u>Purgative Way</u>. In this first stage we spend energy falling down and getting up again. The second stage is the <u>Illuminative Way</u>. We begin to practice more from an enlightened place, even though we still fall down and get up. We are beginning to act with compassion and loving kindness. We are being more mindful, or conscious, of our behavior. The third stage is the <u>Unitive Way</u>. We may experience the Dark Night and have mystical experiences. Notice that we have both very dark and light experiences at this last stage. The poet William Everson, formerly Brother Antoninus, in his book Birth of a Poet, *describes the journey as moving from linear time through a threshold into cyclical time (sacred time) and back to linear time. It is the hero's, the pilgrim's, the seeker's journey.*

Gregory Bateson once said that structure is very important to function. Sometimes structure needs to speed up to support function, and sometimes function needs to slow down to be supported by structure. I view religion as the structure that supports spirituality. My concern about much of spirituality today is that it is not well supported. Many have abandoned their own religious traditions and beliefs seeking the freedom of new age spirituality. I believe that religion (theology) is necessary for good spiritual practice. I believe that spirituality is absolutely necessary for the vibrancy of religion. It is the Pentecost, the coming of the Holy Spirit. Without religion or theology, spirituality is not grounded. Without spirituality, religion is just an organization and will never soar.

This is how, today, I would answer Abbot Robert's question, "What does all this have to do with theology or religion?"

Mediocre–Will George and Dragon Accept the Middle Way?

A therapy client of mine had trouble with his life being in the middle. When he was a child, Bs and Cs were never good enough in his family. As a result, accomplishments were accompanied by the imperative to do better. Celebrating and savoring successes were not practiced in his family. Phrases such as "living up to one's potential," "idleness is the devil's workshop," and "always do your best" were family mantras. After a holiday, he would say, "I enjoyed myself, but I didn't like the time it took to get back on schedule."

Once I was conducting a workshop in which there was a psychiatrist who took his vacation time to attend. During the week, it was quite evident that he was not having fun. He took copious notes and worked hard at learning all he could. His imperative was to "be perfect." I knew that he was Catholic, and he knew that I was an ordained priest. One day I asked him to kneel before me. Placing my hands over his head, I said, "By the power vested in me, I hereby declare you to be perfect." At least for the duration of the workshop, he allowed himself to play and enjoy himself. Hopefully he took home the permission to find his perfection in the mediocre.

The word "mediocre" derives from the Latin "medius," meaning the middle and "ocris," meaning peak. If you are mediocre, you are in the middle of the peak. Your "peak experience" is a middling one. Back in Oklahoma where I grew up, when asked how you were, an acceptable answer was, "Fair to middlin'."

Who told you that perfection exists only at the top?

There is an abundance of perfection right in the middle. Visualize a peak. Peaks are tapered, coming to an apex. It is at that point where there is a shortage of space. If this is the only place of perfection, most of us, most of the time, will not be perfect. Is it like Animal Farm, *where some are more equal than others, more perfect than others?*

The path of the monk is a one based on moderation and on a balanced, measured life. We were not hermits or ascetics, nor did we espouse the poverty of St. Francis. We lived in a community under a rule and an Abbot. The Abbot is a father figure whose role is to serve the community. St. Benedict in Chapter 64 of his *Rule for Monks* instructs the Abbot to measure out justice and mercy. Though written in the fifth century, these instructions apply very much to today's world both for ecclesiastics and other politicians:

"Let him recognize that his goal must be profit for the monks, not preeminence for himself. He must be chaste, temperate and merciful. He should always let mercy triumph over judgment. He must hate faults but love the brothers. When he must punish them, he should use prudence and avoid extremes; otherwise, by rubbing too hard to remove the rust, he may break the vessel. By this we do not mean that he should allow faults to flourish, but rather...he should prune them away with prudence and love as he sees best for each individual. Let him strive to be beloved rather than feared. He should be discerning and moderate, bearing in mind the discretion of holy Jacob, who said: "If I drive my flocks too hard, they will all die in a single day (Gen 33:13). Therefore, drawing on this and other examples of discretion, the mother of virtues, he must so arrange everything that the strong have something to yearn for and the weak nothing to run from."

In Chapter 40, St. Benedict addresses The Proper Amount Of Drink:
"Everyone has his own gift from God, one this and another

that (I Cor 7:7). It is, therefore, with some uneasiness that we specify the amount of food and drink for others. However, with due regard for the infirmities of the sick, we believe that a half bottle of wine a day is sufficient for each. But those to whom God gives the strength to abstain must know that they will earn their own reward. The superior will determine when local conditions, work, or the summer heat indicates the need for a greater amount. He must, in any case, take great care lest excess or drunkenness creep in. We read that monks should not drink wine at all; but since the monks of our day cannot be convinced of this, let us at least agree to drink moderately, and not to the point of excess, 'for wine makes even wise men go astray (Sir 19:2).' However where local circumstances dictate an amount much less than what is stipulated above, or even none at all, those who live there should bless God and not grumble. Above all we admonish them to refrain from grumbling."

The "middle way" requires you, as practitioner, to exercise balance. Not too much, and not too little. "In medio stat virtus." Virtue stands in the middle. This the place of holiness and health. The root word for medicine is "mederi," which means to measure. Health and holiness come from right measure. The measure is an inward process, not the same for everyone. Meditation also comes from the same root. You meditate, center yourself, and measure your breathing. This practice demands lots of wiggle room for freedom and discretion.

What a difficult practice today when you are told that you should have the peak perfect body, marriage, home, car. The "measure-ment" is outside us. Attempting to meet a standard that doesn't fit your insides explains why you and I fail at crash diets. The measure is external instead of internal. Maybe we should eat only when we are hungry and not eat when we are not. What a novel idea!

I am aware that I don't have the "peak perfect" body, marriage, home, or car. My body, marriage, home, and car are middling and perfect. The next time someone asks me how many square feet my house is or how new my car is I'll answer, with measured pride, that my home and car are mediocre and perfect.

Humble Path–Sacred Journey:
George Must Get Off His High Horse to Join Lady Dragon on the Earth

I visited a special friend of mine who was a mentor to many on their spiritual paths. He was dying of cancer. I went to his hospital room, where they were giving him palliative care since death was near. I held his hand as he said to me with anguish in his voice, "George, I don't want to die." I have no memory of my response. I hope I did not say something inept about the "afterlife" or "you will be with God." He already believed these as true. He was about to go through a doorway, passing from ordinary time into cyclical, sacred time. As a mystic, he had gone there often in his years of spiritual practice. Not able to walk because of his illness, he had found a place of balance where he could soar while being trapped in his chair or bed. He knew he was dying, but embraced a full life. Now he was about to lose his balance. He was going to die soon.

Because he was a humble man, he knew that he had to let go.

His trials are lessons of humility for us. Humility is truth. You do not need to deny your physical or emotional strengths, your intellectual acumen. To do this is false humility. Accepting ourselves, while acknowledging our strengths <u>*and*</u> *weaknesses is our practices. Are you able to do this?*

Dying was a continuation of his practice. Hope was abandoning him to despair, faith to doubt, and confidence to fear. Humility and acceptance were to be his only practices to balance despair, doubt, and fear. Those who loved him and the angels of hospice, elders all, were accompanying him to the door leading to the other side. He had to bow his head and pass through on his own. He was afraid of letting go. I held his hand. That was the best I could do.

We use the word "passing" to dress up the word "death." We do pass when we die, and we pass when we are born. I was present when my daughter gave birth to my granddaughter. My wife and I, my son-in-law, my daughter's twin sister, a personal coach for my daughter, a midwife, and nurses filled the room as we witnessed my daughter laboring to bring the baby from a familiar, predictable, safe, and pleasant place into our ordinary time and place. The baby resisted passing through the birth canal, just as my friend had resisted passing through the death canal. Birth, too, is a mystical experience. As the baby presented herself, our tears of joy mixed with the healthy cries of the baby.

Birth, death, and rebirth describe our spiritual path. To recover innate wholeness, we must die to our fragmented self and be reborn. Humility and acceptance are the practices that allow us to let go. We, often through pride, have forgotten who we are. The practice of humility helps us remember. Humility comes from "humus," which means earth. Our spirituality is an earthy, grounded one that prepares us for awe and wonder. The paradox of humility is that it leads to the recognition of our dignity. Pride, even in the practice of humility and spirituality, is dangerous. We need mentors, elders, and rituals to remind us of our truth.

St. Benedict, in the prologue to his Rule *for monks, discusses the attitude he wishes from those who enter the monastic path:*

We are establishing a school of the Lord's service. In this formation we hope not to prescribe anything that is harsh or too heavy. If there is some restriction, it is because reason demands it for the correction of vices and the preservation of love. Do not be frightened by this and desert the way of salvation, because it is narrow only at the beginning. As we make progress in the monastic way of life and in faith, the heart will be enlarged and the way of God's commandments will be run in the extreme sweetness that comes from love (RB Prol.45–49).

In chapter seven of St. Benedict's Rule, *he lists 12 steps of humility. Here they are in summary form:*
1. Make a serious effort to live a good life.
2. Renounce self-will and desire.
3. Submit to a superior in imitation of Christ.
4. Be patient in enduring difficulties with equanimity.
5. Practice self-revelation.
6. Be content with the least of everything.
7. Keep a sharp awareness of one's own liabilities.
8. Avoid individualist and attention-seeking behavior.
9. Practice a radical restraint of speech.
10. Avoid laughter.
11. Speak with gravity and in few words.
12. Show humility in your body and heart.

Chapter seven is one the most difficult chapters for us moderns to digest. It is quite a relief for the monk to read further in the rule that the Abbot is to moderate expectations for monks who cannot live according to the letter of the rule and to support those who can. Monks laugh and appreciate humor! Benedictine monasticism is a way of balance. Moderation in all things, the middle way, is an essential part of the rule.

This idea is also present in Eastern practices: The Buddha was walking along a river one day when a very excited old man came running up to him exclaiming, "Master, I have finally achieved life long goal. I can walk across the river on top of the water." The Buddha looked at him sadly and said, "It is too bad you have wasted so much time. You could have used the bridge."

Zen master Shunryu Suzuki, in his book Zen Mind Beginner's Mind *writes, "Zen is not some kind of excitement, but concentration on our usual everyday routine."*

The passage into life and death is narrow. So is the doorway into sacred space and time. You who have experienced a sweat in Native American tradition will recall that to enter the sweat lodge you must crawl through the opening and continue clockwise around the fire pit to find your place. This humble entry reminds you that you are entering sacred space. You need special care and protection to go through the Shaman's doorway, letting go of ego and passing into extraordinary time and space. You are accompanied by the archetypes: Elder, Lover, Magician, and Warrior. All directions and elements are invoked for your journey: East, South, West, and North—Air, Fire, Water, and Earth. Armed and balanced, you begin your spiritual journey.

Conspiracies of loving people, also on your path, are there to support your passing. Sacred space is a place where it is OK to be who you are, letting go of ego, accepted warts and all. The proper attitude for this journey, from beginning to end, is humility. Midwifed into sacred time and space as a baby is at birth, you also need your hand held at death.

Living on the Margin – George and Dragon at the Edge of the Cave: Darkness Meets Light

Survival and creativity are edges or margins where we live. In survival, we experience scarcity, in creativity, abundance.

I have been observing my granddaughter who, at three months, needs to be fed, held, physically and emotionally supported, protected, and accepted. Without these, she would literally dry up and die. She is dependent on my daughter, son in law, and her grandparents to provide what she requires. In those relationships she experiences abundant loving acceptance. What a joy to see her now, at three years, grow into her own creativity in such an environment! She is living at both her survival and creative margins.

All of us continue to need nurturing elements in our lives. Like a baby, we depend on receiving what our physical and psychological beings demand, and we are hungry for wholeness and creativity. When we live only in survival, we go from fix to fix, meal to meal, drink to drink, job to job, medication to medication, lover to lover, attempting to fill our hunger for more.

Hunger can only be quenched when we are in union with our integrated reality, connected to our creative, spiritual selves. If we are not in that union, our seeking becomes addiction. We live as if we were in a deep pool tethered to a rock that rests on the bottom. The tether allows us to barely raise our noses to the top. We gasp for air and remain bound, believing there is no exit from the pool. "If it were not for this weight that holds me, I would be free." In survival we reach out for anything that might, even momentarily, satisfy us or, at least, make survival less painful. Those living on the survival margin continue to hope for rescue from their plight.

When I was business manager of our monastery and small college, I helped create the first budget for our educational institution. Traditionally we monks ran our finances out of a cigar box. We spent whatever was in the box. When the box was empty, we did without or performed additional work for funds. As we got in the college business, we could not function so simply. We hired a "development director," a fundraiser, who promised to bring $100,000 to our coffers. We naively believed him, put that income into the budget, and encumbered those funds. He was not successful in raising the money. We fired him and were $100,000 deeper in our debt pool. We were losing touch with our monastic creative abundance, becoming defined by a survival budget, refugees in the business world.

We too may have lost our way. We cannot solve enough problems on the survival edge or margin to bring us home to our spiritual selves. We must go there first. We need to discover that we can untie ourselves from the rock. It does not have us. We have it. In the process of recovery, we decide that the pain of holding on becomes greater than the fear of letting go. We let go and surface to our creative edge. We come out of the darkness and allow ourselves to be exposed and free. From the place of enlightenment (consciousness), we can reconnect to our authentic self and to each other in relationships that are whole. We bring creativity and spirituality to our eating, pleasure, work, and sexuality.

A woman whom I saw in therapy with her husband was recovering from serious depression. Her husband had been her rescuer. He had grown accustomed to taking care of her, and she was accustomed to being the identified patient. Once she began her recovery and she stopped taking all the drugs he was administering to her, she became aware of the abuse that she suffered from him. She decided not to hide and protect herself by staying depressed. He in turn increased his abusive behavior to keep the old system working. Ultimately, she had to divorce him to get on with her life.

To what are you tethered, surviving instead of thriving? What are your addictions? What are your excuses? What pain are you suffering by holding on? What are your fears of letting go? Just let go!

The Edge–George and Dragon: No Place to Hide

The Desert

My wife Carol and I returned to the desert where we spent Holy Week until after sunrise on Easter morning. We retreated to a place where we heard little news, a cleansing place, restful and quiet. It was time for us to leave the war stress and political turmoil experienced by all of us. Carol, a photographer, looks for light and shadows that play against changing forms of landscape, rocks, and cactus. I search for a place to meditate, think, read, and write. I was conscious of resorts, golf courses, and houses where people have transformed the desert instead of the desert transforming them. I noticed the edges where these structures meet the desert, community meeting solitude, solitude meeting community; both dramatically defining where one starts and the other ends; profane abutting the sacred.

Terry Tempest Williams, in her book, Red *writes: "If the desert is holy, it is because it is a forgotten place that allows us to remember the sacred. Perhaps that is why every pilgrimage to the desert is a pilgrimage to the self. There is no place to hide and so we are found."*

We found ourselves. We honored our separateness as Carol wandered off seeking subjects of her photographs. I discovered a place in the desert that suited my needs. When we came together in the early evening, we were refreshed and enjoyed our time together over a glass of wine by the fire.

Physical Edges

My daughters once took a self-defense course. It was described as follows: "This course is unique in that the students learn many skills in which to defend themselves in situations which may be anything from verbal to physical abuse. They learn skills such as boundary setting, de-escalation and physical techniques with a full contact defense."

What a moving experience it was for me to see my daughters scream out "No!" to an attacker, a man who was not holding back his abusive thrust. The attacker was well-padded. My girls were not. I was frightened for them, angry with the man who was assaulting them, and was absolutely amazed that my Sarah and Jennifer, my 17-year-old twins, could kick a man as large as I in the groin with a 30-pound force. This, as the attacker told me later, was quite sufficient to knock any man to his knees and might even knock him out.

Since that event, I view my daughters differently. They defended their boundaries, their edges, and met their assailant. They are powerful women, posturing themselves in such a way as to demand respect not letting themselves, to the best of their abilities, be victims. One of the instructors told us about an experiment that involved men who had been imprisoned for assault and rape. The men were in a situation where they could not communicate with each other, but they independently picked the same woman that they would attack. This woman presented herself as a potential victim by her posture and aura of low self-esteem. She had forgotten who she was.

Protecting yourself from what is not wanted is important. You also need to establish boundaries and meeting places for what you do want. It is necessary, when boundaries are violated, to powerfully persuade the assailant to back off and go away. It is also necessary to establish boundaries or margins for relational contact: "Stay," "Talk to me," "Listen to me," "Touch me," meeting toe-to-toe, face-to-face, getting ready for what you do want!

Do you live at your creative edges, finding yourself where there is no place to hide?

In the Box–George and Dragon Dilemma: Being Right or Tending to Their Relationship

I remember years ago at the beginning of the baseball season when my twin daughters were ten. We arrived two hours before the As game in Oakland. My daughters, and maybe the young boy in me, came early to watch batting practice and get autographs of McGuire and Canseco, the home run heroes of that time. Finding a parking place close to the entrance gate, we eagerly passed through the turnstile, only to he accosted by a security person demanding to search my backpack. Unwittingly I was carrying four or five cans of soda because I wanted to avoid the high prices charged inside the park. With an authoritative voice, the guard said we were not allowed in with the contraband. I accepted the decision as he took our sodas and placed them in a box by the gate. We went inside the park. We watched batting practice and got autographs.

With still time to spare, we returned to the gate. There I asked the guard if I could take the sodas out of the box to our car I had parked just a few yards from where we stood. I pointed out to him that it was the blue Volvo next to the green Chevy.

"Nope," he said, "once it's in the box, it's confiscated."

I protested that it would only take a minute for us to reach the car and return. Again, he repeated, "If it's in the box, it's confiscated." As rage rose inside me, I looked at him, now standing with other guards who were enjoying themselves, laughing at my seemingly ridiculous request. I felt as if was in the box, powerless, angry, feeling trapped. I knew that I was being abused.

As in Sartre's play *No Exit,*, I experienced existential anxiety. I began to perspire, forgetting to give myself room to breathe. I almost created a scene that I would later regret. Fortunately I glanced to my right where my daughters stood waiting, both likely embarrassed. I instantly remembered that I loved them, I remembered that I was their father and why we came that day. I took their hands as we returned to our seats to enjoy the game.

Jargon has it that we are to "think outside the box." This phrase seems to invite creativity by not letting us be bound by ordinary patterns that define our thoughts, values, feelings, and behavior. Once we are outside the box, as the theory implies, we are free to question old patterns and make choices, even if it is to choose the situations by which we are defined: aging, suffering, or imprisonment. We freely choose them. We have them; they do not have us. From the liberated place, we might design new possibilities. When we practice this in relationships, we are free to make new choices together. Great theory and a difficult practice!

When I was a Benedictine monk at the age of 23, at the height of my sexuality yet vowed to celibacy, I experienced myself in a very enclosed box. I determined that it was not right for me to have sexual thoughts. We used to define them as impure thoughts. The more I tried not to have them, the more I did have them, or they me. Full of guilt, I took these sins to my confessor and spiritual counselor, who happened to be my professor in moral theology and canon (church) law. He was a very wise and holy man. After hearing my pain and struggle with my dilemma, he said to me: "Remember the Law is for the person, not the person for the Law." What I understood that to mean was that all laws are designed to help us be who we truly are, whole, not fragmented people, and to help us in relationships.

The purpose of rules and laws are to be supportive, not restrictive. The spirit of the law is far more important than the letter of the law. Jesus of the New Testament came to fulfill the law. His message is one of freedom, love, and forgiveness. Sometimes we forget that and act as if laws are meant to control behavior. We let ourselves be "confiscated" in boxes because we are trying of avoid what we fear. We remain in boxes (relationships) because we accept what happens there as familiar, predictable, safe, and painful, a pain we know.

When I turned and saw my daughters and the looks on their faces, thank God, I chose freedom, discerned what I did want from what I did not want, got outside the box, and enjoyed the game.

George and daughters Sarah & Jennifer

Discernment

We experience a survival crisis when we are in the throes of being consumed, abandoned, rejected, or abused, and when we are ill, failing, aging, or dying. Survival dictates that we choose either to succumb to or separate from the forces that constrain us. We cannot separate enough from what we do not want to have a relationship with what we do want. Trying not to be "codependent" does not prepare anyone for a relationship. It leaves us "safe" and disconnected.

Discernment elicits another kind o freedom: a freedom for rather than from. It is freedom chosen in a creative crisis. Instead of fleeing the scene of polarities, e.g. fear and excitement, despair, and hope; we embrace both poles. We remember who we are and were before we, bound by survival forces, forgot, Meditative practices, therapy, loving and being loved unconditionally, near death experiences, and other profound events help us recover who we are. From that remembering, we differentiate and choose what we want to keep and what we want to let go as we move on. We find our freedom in ourselves first, and from that sacred place we relate to both sides of the opposites in our lives. Health and illness, living and dying are relational experiences. We are free in the presence of the dualities. The cross, in Christian tradition, is a symbol of freedom found in suffering.

Paul, a client of mine, is an artist. He is one of the most creative men I have known, a dreamer who composes beautiful lyrics and music. He contacts me when he is in a depressed state. He has multiple physical maladies. The most painful is a problem with his colon. He cannot relieve himself for days. This problem, along with others, causes him to be depressed and unable to complete his work or carry on a successful intimate relationship. I asked him to tell me a story about his debilitating Illnesses. He described it as a curse. I asked him to explain how this "curse" functions in his life. He told me it keeps him from being free to go public with his music, complete some CDs, and earn money. He often, with passion, described his music to me and, with a depressed voice, would tell me how impossible it was to bring his music to fruition. This is Paul who survives between his curse and his great promise as an artist.

The person who is debilitated by the curse and who is called to create by his great talents is Paul the Hero. He, as hero, creates even when he is practically debilitated. He still writes songs about the lover with a broken heart who gives his life for the beloved. This is the Paul that is available for healing and healthy relationships. I made a contract with him as one hero to another. I found it helpful to tell him my own heroic journey of success and failure, health and illness. I will share my writing with him if he completes a CD with his lyrics set to his music played on an acoustic guitar. He resonated to this contract. He still has his depression and physical ailments. The Paul who is more than those ailments is free to be who he is and will live up to his calling. It will be interesting to see if he will not need his colon problem or his depression. The agreement between us is a challenge for me to be who I am, more than a therapist, and keep my contract. The two of us will prevail

There is a gestalt principle that states, "We don't change what we don't first embrace." By separating ourselves, we attempt to end what we don't want. That leaves a void in our life we often try to fill with the very material that we didn't want, e.g., repeating familiar, predictable, safe, and painful relationships. Even if we do find the just-right lover or job, we may not be ready for the relationship because we have unfinished business with what we do not want. Quantum physics and David Bohm tell us, "The whole is what is." When we try to separate from anything in our lives, we are violating another principle of modern physics, non separability, which states that wholes cannot be dissected.

Instead of attempting psychological or spiritual surgery upon the negatives in our lives, our task is to stand between the poles of positives and negatives and feel the tension there while focusing on how the relationship is present in us, not as duality but as paradox. Gregory Bateson's definition of a paradox as a "set of opposites in which case we choose both," is appropriate here. The way to get ready for the paradox is to acknowledge, not to solve, but to embrace it.

Changing our lives and the directions that we choose are secondary. First we must enter into the relationship, empower all "sets of opposites" that exist in our lives, honor them, and from there continue in the direction that we have discerned. We stand between weakness and strength and feel the tension. From our true selves we practice being loving and compassionate to ourselves and others struggling in survival. Freedom lies between hope and despair. We find our power in that place. To risk being free for the more that exists for us, we need to stop trying to be free from whatever binds us. The true self is a profound self that taps into the more. The ego self is a survival self. What binds the ego self might be hope that the context in which we live will change: that we get well, find a job, find the right person to share our lives. What binds the ego self might be the despair that we will never have what we want. The polarity of hope and despair pulls at us from opposing directions, and sometimes we vacillate from one to other, depending on circumstances. What a humbling experience! We must ask our deeper selves <u>what every set of opposites in our lives needs from us?</u> Our healing begins when the self is free and creative, accepting paradoxes, not separating from them.

My friend Don was a man about my age who once was a very fine athlete and coach. He suffered from MS. I visited him after a long interval of absence. As I arrived at his house, I must admit I was apprehensive of what I might find. He was a man who reminded me of myself. He relied on his physical size and strength to carry him through the trials present in the exertion associated with athletics. I now know that I avoided contacting him because of what might happen to me if I lost my physical prowess.

As I approached his door, I feared what I might meet in myself as I visited him. I fumbled with the latch to his front gate and heard his booming voice from inside the house asking if I could handle the latch and to come in. Don, still a powerful-looking man but supported by frozen legs, stood and welcomed me. He slowly shuffled across the room as I reached out to him. Thank God we had made our first contact! The ostensible reason (or excuse) for getting together was to drink some wines that he had collected. On his dining table were glasses and three bottles of cabernet. He forced himself into a chair on one side of the table, I on the other. For three hours we tasted wines and explored his world of illness and health and my world of illness and health.

Toward the end of the evening we both emphatically recognized the blessing of his journey. He knew he was seriously ill and that he would get worse and die of this disease. He hoped that there would be a cure for MS, but he also knew how quickly he was failing and so was unlikely to see the cure. He had chosen to live with this hope and knowledge. Brother David Stender-Rast, a spiritual writer, has said that this is all we need to do: "Live now-Live fully now-Get ready to die." Don and I were doing just that as we sipped our wine, laughed, discussed literature, philosophy, spirituality, illness, and death. What a relief it was to not be in denial. I walked away from my evening with Don feeling freer than I have in a long time.

AIDs victim William Bettellyoun wrote, "When you have a terminal illness, you either have hope or freedom. I've chosen freedom. I try to live for the day" (Kafka). I would phrase it a bit differently. When you have a terminal illness, you choose a place central to both hope and despair. Feeling and accepting the tension between the two, you find yourself and choose freedom.

Woundedness & Change

I repeat my story about John (cf. Introduction) who had been sober for a number of years, very active in AA, and a sponsor for others in the program. I asked him during one of our sessions, "Who else are you besides being an alcoholic?"

He replied, "I don't know. I have never asked myself that question. I believe that if I let myself accept that I am something more than an alcoholic, I might go hack to drinking."

His words have stayed with me as I meet many who are "wounded children" who come from dysfunctional families who exhibit addictive behavior or are adult children of alcoholics. Many of these are in recovery of one sort or another, and most are involved in the Twelve Step Program. I ask them the same question that I asked John and receive similar answers. Many have denied the fact of their addiction or that they have been abused as children.

Work needs to be done to release the anger, guilt, and sadness that bind the person to the past. I wonder if, like John, many fear letting go of what they have done to themselves or what was done to them, and thereby prevent them from being more than that which is familiar, predictable, safe, and painful. I am reminded of two stories: A woman in my therapy group announced that she wanted to work on her anger towards her grandmother. I agreed. She began to beat on a pillow screaming and venting her rage. After a few minutes, I told her that I thought she couldn't be angry enough to get her grandmother to change, especially since what happened was long ago and her grandmother was dead. Once she accepted that anger was her painful way of staying attached to the past, she was able to let go.

A man guilty for the sins he had committed went to confession to a priest who heard the man's sins, absolved him and gave him a penance. The man became angry at the priest for not giving him enough penance for the "terrible" sins he had committed. The priest <u>reduced</u> his penance. The man called him a terrible priest, not fit to hear his confession. The priest said to him that if he didn't get the hell out of the confessional, he wouldn't give him any penance at all!

When someone stays stuck in a feeling state, gets strokes for feeling that feeling, uses that feeling as a reason not to change, or uses that feeling to justify certain behaviors, that feeling is a racket.

Bob and Mary Goulding, authors of Changing Lives through Redecision Therapy, *were my mentors who helped me let go and seek what was possible for me. I quote from their book as they discuss "rackets."*

"...The racket is simply the chronic, stereotyped unpleasant feeling. The feelings are used to attempt to change others. At times of course, people do what we want, if we suffer enough. All of us have had the experience of having been sad or angry at someone-spouse, child, parent, and boss -and of that person then changing his behavior. Extortion is the term we give to the use of rackets in an attempt to modify someone else's behavior.

Parents teach children about rackets. Mother or father says, 'you make me so angry when you slam the door. You make me so happy when you pee-pee in the toilet.' The child is thus told that he is responsible for the parental feelings. He grows up believing that he makes people feel. Does he ever ask himself what they were angry, nervous or anxious about before he entered the scene? Rackets are used in other ways also. If someone is in a suicidal script, for instance, and has at one time decided he can always kill him-self if things get too bad, he'll save up his bad feel-ings, collecting them as if he were trading stamps so that, when he has "enough" stamps he can kill him-self. Such stamps can be produced in a number of ways. He can play games in which he ends up being kicked and feeling sad. He can look around to see what the bad news is today, such as the war in Lebanon or the rising inflation. He can lie in bed at night, remembering all the sad things that ever hap-pened to him. He remembers that Mother never loved him or Father never played with him. He can spend his therapy hours dredging up sadder and sadder memories. In order to feel sad enough, he may even fantasize that his wife is unfaithful even when there is no evidence for believing this" (pp. 33–34).

The Gouldings taught thousands of therapists the techniques of Redecision Therapy. They taught others and me how to capture the "creative free child, the little professor" and from that place in each of us to redecide about how to be and how to feel. It is from that place that we are free to change. There is a danger in hanging out in the "wounded child." We may simply learn how to survive with other "wounded children." I often quip, "The family that is depressed together, stays together." That is true for anger and anxiety.

Once I had a practice in an office above another ther-apist who was practicing downstairs. It seems that most of the time this therapist's clients were dealing with anger issues. Loud noises, screaming, beating sounds, and general pandemonium would emanate up through the floor into my office. I began to question my own work since I was not elic-iting such explosions. It was only later that I discovered that the therapist had many anger issues that the therapist's clients echoed or expressed for the therapist.

It is difficult to let go of behaviors or feelings that are familiar, predictable, safe, and painful. If we are going to reach out to what is possible, we must experiment with that. Even before we let go of the old script or story about ourselves, I believe we need to experiment with the new story. It is at this level that we need one another in order to "push the envelope" and experiment with a new story. Even before this new place is completely perfected (the task of the rest of our life), we can begin now to collect evidence in our hearts, minds, and bodies about how we can flourish there. While just as in recovery, only we ourselves have to change, so also in order to move to this new place, we have creative crises, where we can return to survival or move on. We experiment before the decision because we need this new evidence of the possible (creative) support system and let go of the survival support system.

After we decide, then we exercise our decision, keep on deciding. We are victims no longer. We become seekers of the possible. We look for new metaphor. In the chapter of this book titled Conversion, *I quote Gregory Bateson, an important mentor of mine. His words are worth repeating because they relevant here. Bateson said, "Our grasp exceeds our reach, or what's a meta-phor." Metaphor is a place where we listen to new messages about being and feeling.*

We can increase the frame of life and make it possible to literally change our way of living and to do all those things that we have put off because of shortages of money or energy and create a place of abundance. How do we get ready for abundance? We know how to get ready for shortage! On the literal level we may breathe more, love more, touch more, and risk more. Because we can risk believing that we have more, it is literally possible for us to give more to the relationship with our lover and those that we love. The experiment at this level is to act as if we have what it takes to give what we want. This is not pretending, because we base our acting on the evidence we detect in our being and feeling.

We create metaphorically what is possible. We dream more. Gregory Bateson reminds us that "Neurotics need to dream more, and psychotics need to know the difference." We laugh more because we see in larger contexts and are not so myopic as survivors tend to be. We see the humor in life, our own foibles, and those of others. We take it all less seriously. We listen to more music and read more poetry, even when the news of the world is so terrible on the 6 o'clock television rendition. There is always more! Because we embrace the more, we are able to accept that life comes to us and is experienced paradoxically. Bateson defined a paradox as, "A set of opposites in which case we choose both." We, from our enlarged frame and from the abundance we experience, are able to say yes to feel both love and hate at the same time. We can want to be close and distant at the same time. We can even want to live and die at the same time.

We Are One – George and Dragon United

I remember a "Pogo" cartoon in which he says, "We have met the enemy and he is us." It is important to not see our enemies as ourselves, because we need to hate in order to kill. If we see others as us, we might love them instead.

Beatrice Bruteau used the image of a rose to explain that in our depths we are united. Roses have many petals and tips. Like the rose, we, at out tips appear to be separate, individual beings. She calls this "tip consciousness."

"In tip consciousness we experience being outside of one another, over against one another, in need of one another, and potentially hostile to one another. As we descend down the petal we notice that the petals overlap............ The one and the many coexist as the whole. At some point, our consciousness becomes aware of this systematic aspect of our finite existence. I believe that on some level or (levels) we are always aware of it, but our reflexive consciousness just doesn't bring it to explicit, or rational, consciousness. We live in terms of great symbiosis, but don't often think about it or discuss it....... This is the place deep inside where we are one. At first limited to the tight short circuit of the reflexive consciousness at the tip of the petal my "I" gradually extends to take in more and more of 'my' petal which inevitably includes more and more of "your" petals because of the overlapping. When I say "I" therefore, I come to mean more and more of the whole.........I remember who I am, that I am unlimited personal being totally outpouring into all the rest of you, as you in turn are doing. We are all one, in our infinitude and in our finitude and as between our infinitude and our finitude" (pp. 292–295).

We, as we increase our consciousness, remember who we are. Sometimes we must literally get this memory back into our members, our body. Our minds forget, so do our bodies. My granddaughter, age one, had not forgotten. I was helping her walk down our hallway to a mirror at the end of the hall. As she approached the mirror, she kissed her reflection. I thought, at that moment, narcissism is fine at age one. Her "I" was kissing "I" What is her sense of self? Later on she may be taught not to be selfish, to think of others. I hope that she continues to learn to love others as herself, to have this "I"-"I" relationship. We have to remember that we are one.

William Johnston in *The Still Point* quotes Dr. Akihisa Kondo, a Japanese therapist: "After a number of interviews I asked a patient of mine who was very much concerned that she was an illegitimate child (and who had been sitting according to my instructions), 'Who were you before you were an illegitimate child?' She looked puzzled for an instant, then, suddenly, burst into tears, crying out, "I am I! Oh, I am I" (p. 61).

Our work goes on. Once we have a sense of non-duality and accept our unity, our spiritual practice is to also let go of our concept of "I." There is a Gestalt therapy principal stating that we do not let go of what we do not accept. Accepting our unity and community is a major step along our spiritual path.

Because we have community, stability, and love, we are better able, alone, to deepen our individual practice. Sometimes we forget this and need help remembering from our relationships. St. George meets Lady Dragon at the mouth of the cave, then each may enter the cave of the heart where all duality ceases and they are truly one: "I" loving "I." "We met the enemy and the enemy is us."

Creative and Sacred Space –
A Place of Union and Communion

"Abandon hope all you who enter here."
Entrance to Dante's Inferno

"Renew hope all you who enter here."
Entrance to Creative and Sacred Space

Here we are. You did not recognize your precious gifts and forget who you are. I, too, have done that. I join you in this sacred place where we are invited to remember who we are and come to our precious creative edges. The entrance is narrow and sometimes difficult to pass through. Not unlike being born and dying, we travel from ordinary to a sacred time and a sacred place. I invite you to accompany me as we renew our hope. I will guide you, dear reader, as we begin our journey. Let's take the first step and enter.

Once inside, marvel at the majestic structure! I experience this sacred space as a cathedral whose walls reach to the heavens. Light shining through gothic-framed windows warms us as we stand in the sanctuary. Recognize this as a place of freedom to be who you are. Feeling awe and wonder, let's create a shared vision of the possible. Here our spirits can soar.

Virgil, Roman poet and author of *The Aeneid*, accompanied Dante as he entered hell. He led Dante into the depths that included those who committed the seven deadly sins: Pride, Envy, Wrath, Sloth, Greed, Gluttony and Lust. Dante placed classical poets, philosophers, politicians, and ecclesiastics of history and of his own time into his descending circles of hell.

You and I have someone to accompany us as well. Thomas Merton, a Trappist monk, mystic, and scholar walks with us as we explore Creative and Sacred Space. All who enter here are practitioners of Mindfulness and Loving Kindness and are Peacemakers, Pure of heart, Those who weep, Poor in spirit, Merciful, Meek, those who Hunger and Thirst for Justice and Suffer Persecution for Justice's sake. Merton points out some whom we might expect to see here: Moses, Jesus, Buddha, and Mohammed. There is Our Lady of Guadalupe. Over here are saints Francis, Benedict, Teresa of Avila, Therese of Lisieux, and Mother Theresa. There are others, certainly not "plaster saints:" Archbishop Oscar Romero of El Salvador, Martin Luther King, Cesar Chavez, John and Bobby Kennedy, and Pope John XXIII.

Merton asks us to focus not only on those whom we might expect, but see those whom he calls the "marginal people." There are the poor, downtrodden, and hungry who continue their creative dance. They will not be victims! Here are poets, creating songs of protest and confrontation. I am surprised to see Allen Ginsberg.

Merton tells us that not all in Sacred Space have died. Many come here often and return to their earthly work. The Dalai Llama comes often, as do other mystics who follow their spiritual paths. He reminds us that we are all meant to be part of this community. Jimmy and Rosalyn Carter are frequent visitors.

These are some of the community that I saw. Whom did you see?

Even though we may not spend many of our days here, and even though our survival cares draw us away, we always know this place exists. Know this, because we meet here on occasion. Enter with reverence, because this is a sanctuary, a tabernacle containing **presence** created by our love. With as much of our being as possible, we listen to what each brings as offering. Together, we are edified, built up by sharing our stories. Practicing loving kindness (compassion), mindfulness, and giving thanks for our blessing, we respond to needs both physical and spiritual. We tend to each other. There is a story from the Far East that in hell (Dante's *Inferno*) people have chopsticks one yard long so they cannot possibly reach their mouths. In heaven (Sacred Space) chopsticks are also one yard long. But here, people feed one another.

Spirituality is relationship. We are one with everyone and everything in creation. Imitate the Native Americans who, after each prayer or song sung in a Sweat Ceremony, remember "all our relations." Pray for peace and healing of the planet. We have set ourselves aside from our ordinary life. We have offered up and have been offered in the name of love. We have celebrated our atonement, our at-one-ment.

Together in love, we prepare our place for the **more**. Open to what is possible, we, sharing in a larger Self, are available for mystical experiences in this together place.

St. Gregory's abbey chapel

Stage III: Choosing–Synthesis
Good-bye to Denis

I visited my former monastery many times over the last 36 years. The first time I went back was in 1979. Abbot Adrian, a new Abbot, and the monk who succeeded me in my role as business manager, responded to my letter congratulating him on being elected and asked if I could come to visit. This was his response, very different from that which I had received from Abbot Robert:

St. Gregory's Abbey

Shawnee, Oklahoma 74801

April 5, 1979

Dear George & Carol

Thank you for your letter of congratulations and information. I appreciate the kind words and certainly need your prayers.

It has taken me a while to change the way I think and to accept the fact. For the first couple of weeks I just couldn't even think of myself as Abbot. It is beginning to come a little easier.

I find no reason why you should not visit us. In fact, I want to make the invitation more positive. Please do come and visit us. Most everyone here remembers your fine work for us over several years. And further, we cannot deny our roots but should grow by using all that is good in our past. And I hope we represent something good that you want to remember.

I have heard of families being in a hurry to have their family, but rushing into things with twins is a novel approach. I pray they will be healthy and that grandma and grandpa won't have to wait too long to see them.

Adrian

When I arrived at the Abbey, I noticed that Mass was taking place in the chapel so I went inside, remaining in the rear pew to avoid being noticed. I was surprised when either Abbot Adrian left the altar during the Mass or sent one of the monk-priests to invite me into the sanctuary to join them around the altar. I was so moved by this I don't remember who led me to the altar. I did know by such a loving invitation that I was welcomed.

I have returned to the monastery many times over the years, sometimes by myself, and sometimes with Carol and my daughters, Jennifer and Sarah. We have made a visit to the monastery an important part of our Oklahoma visit with my relatives.

I recall another notable time I returned to my former monastery, St. Gregory's. The abbey sits out on the prairie about 40 miles east of Oklahoma City. It is possible to see the towers of St. Gregory's for many miles. The main building is a very tall Tudor Gothic structure whose towers strain against the sky and remain sturdy even when the tornadoes sweep across the fields. The reason for going there was to celebrate Father Matthew's 50th anniversary as a priest. I was in for a surprise!

After I shared breakfast with Brother Kevin, I took a walk about the grounds to see how the trees I planted 39 years ago had grown, now tall enough to offer much-needed shade. I turned to face the south wind and remembered times from the past when I had to lean into the wind to get where I was going. I spotted a robin and, much to my surprise, a cardinal, scurrying below the branches. As I stood in front of the chapel, a man drove up in his car and stopped to talk to me. I had seen him earlier and had noticed he needed a cane to walk. After saying his name was Mark, he told me that he had also talked to Kevin this morning and heard from him that I had been a monk here. I told him that my monastic years were a long time ago, but I returned when I got the chance. He confided to me that he was an alcoholic and saw Brother Kevin for spiritual guidance.

"I used to see Father Denis," he said. "He had a rough outside but a soft inside."

I agreed with him, but said that Denis was dead and gone now. "No he isn't, he's still here," Mark emphatically replied. As I heard this, I began to cry. Unable to stop, I said good-bye to Mark, who drove away.

I wept deeply over Denis's grave and over all the other monks whose names are on the small crosses. These men: Denis, John, Joe, Eloi, Francis, and others have etched themselves on my heart. I had not realized how deeply I experienced them 'til I stood in the cemetery where I had been so many times.

I helped dig some of the graves. Many years ago, we had to move them to build our new monastery on and near the site of the former cemetery. Saint Benedict, the founder of the Benedictine Order, encouraged his monks to keep death before their eyes. As we moved the remains of the monks, we remembered this injunction. These thoughts rushed upon my memory as I contemplated the monks that helped me on my journey. Each of them gave me precious gifts. All these monks were my monastic brothers. The monks that studied theology and were ordained priests were also called "Father."

Denis

He was a man of slight build and wiry. He had dark hair and piercing eyes. I considered him to be the most intelligent one in our community. When I was a student, Father Denis once told us that if he had not become a monk, he would have become a homeless person, a bum. He taught me what it meant to be an earthy, not a plastic, monk. The local bishop came to our monastery to ordain one of our monks. During the ceremony Denis whispered to me that the monsignor, acting as the bishop's master of ceremonies, providing him cotton to wipe his fingers after the anointing process, was the "man with the cotton balls." He taught me to appreciate Oklahoma. We would play a game of "Do you know where Wetumka (Oklahoma) is or where Nowata is?" He taught me to value intellectual pursuits, encouraged me to read, and complimented me when I wrote. He also let me into that soft compassionate place inside his cryptic exterior. I loved Denis, and I believe he loved me.

Having begun this process of weeping, I continued. Here was John's grave.

John

Father John was a short man who made up for it by being intimidating. He was quite brilliant and creative. He was an athlete, coach, demanding geometry teacher, and a builder. Father John was my football coach when I was in high school. He was a character that I compared to Knute Rockne. He helped me push my boundaries when I did not think that I had it in me. When we were building our monastery, he was the boss on the project. He drove us just as he did the football team. I remembered the strong hate-love feelings for him.

I graduated from St. Gregory's High School, a boarding school conducted by the monks. The motto of the school was "Builder of Men." After graduation I attended Oklahoma A&M College. In my speech class, I wrote and gave speeches about Father John. I attribute my entering the monastery to my relationship with him.

Joe

Father Joe was an Irish storyteller, actor, and comedian. Part of the monk's habit is a scapular that hangs both in front and back from the shoulders, Father Joe loved to dramatically toss his front scapular over his shoulder as he began his class. This ritual was a sign for us to be alert. He was not averse to throwing an eraser at a student who didn't pay attention. He gave me a love of history. He not only taught the events, but laced his teachings with rich stories and humor, too. In the late 1940s and early '50s, my father would drive to

St. Gregory's from my hometown near Tulsa to bring me home during vacations. I looked forward to sharing the latest Father Joe story with my dad. Father Joe had been the principal of the boarding school. A distant cousin of mine, Harry, managed to get himself expelled from St. Gregory's for various deviant behaviors. After kicking him out of school, Father Joe would be convinced by Harry's sister to let him return. Evidently this process happened many times. Father Joe, even in his last days, would retell the stories about Harry. Denis was also very close to Joe. Denis once told me after Joe's death, after reading something exciting or experiencing something stimulating, he would say to himself, "I've got to tell Joe about that." Then he would remember that Joe was dead.

Eloi

Father Eloi was a Basque priest-monk who loved to shock us. He was white-haired and rotund. I remember the time he, at 80-something, went swimming, nude, in our school pool. He lay floating on his back, propelling himself with ping-pong paddles, singing all the while!

Francis

Brother Francis was the oldest monk in the monastery. I believe he was in his 90s when he died. He would tell stories about the early years of the monks in Oklahoma. I heard him tell about the time the monks gave sanctuary to Billy the Kid when he was being pursued by the law. I don't know whether this story or others were true, but he knew how to tell them!

These men were important in my life, and I doubt if I had mourned my loss of them 'til that day. I felt so good after emptying this dammed-up place in me. Now I know why I had to return to St. Gregory's this time. A crippled, alcoholic angel named Mark reminded me to mourn them and to remember that they are still there.

Stability

I traveled to the Abbey about every two years since that initial return in 1979. These journeys have been important to me to complete the unfinished business within myself where I had not fully integrated my monastic past with my current life. I would awake feeling fearful, sad, and fragmented from frequent monastic dreams in which I couldn't remember certain rituals, what passages to read, forgot how to say Mass.

Each time I traveled to Shawnee, I recaptured more of my wholeness. In 1995 when I arrived in Oklahoma City on my way to St. Gregory's in Shawnee, I visited the site of the Murrah Federal Building, which was bombed in April of that year. They were still looking for bodies in the rubble. I was deeply moved by the dedicated reverence of those performing the search. Somehow being there reminded me that I was also looking for myself under the layers, definitions, of whom I had become.

In September of 2001, after the horrendous destruction of the World Trade Center in New York City, I take another trip to Shawnee, again seeking some meaning. I land in Oklahoma City, rent a car and drive the short distance east on Interstate 40 to spend the day and night at St. Gregory's. As I arrive, I do what I ordinarily do every time I return to the monastery: I visit the cemetery to see who died since I was there last. James and Victor lie in the most recent graves, marked by simple concrete crosses with their names on them. James, I had known was near death, and therefore no surprise. Victor's death is another matter. He was young. I'll ask the Abbot what happened to him. Even in the presence of death it's good to be here. In the midst of all the uncertainty and fear that exists outside, here, at the monastery is an island of stability.

The monks vow to be of this Abbey, taking root here. They pray and work, live and die. The Abbot invites me to attend Vespers, the evening prayer. This is the first time since I left the monastery in 1971 that I have been asked to go with the monks into chapel and into the choir stalls to pray. I feel naked as I walk with them. They are in their habits or robes, I am in my tee shirt and trousers. What I notice is that I don't know what to do with my hands as I follow in line. The monks put theirs under their scapulars that hang down in the front and back, covering their robes.

Even with my discomfort, I feel honored as I bow to my partner and find my place in choir. We recite and sing psalms together. At the conclusion of prayer we sing the *Salve Regina*. Charles, a gray-bearded monk, helps me find the text in a prayer book. After Vespers, Charles tells me that he is disappointed that I didn't know the Latin for that song, sung every day in the monastery. He reminds me that I taught him Latin some 40 years ago.

Time is different in the monastery. Forty years is yesterday, today, and tomorrow. Outside, in the world, we measure time by events: today's news and yesterday's news. In the monastery, we sing the *Salve Regina* in Latin after Vespers. It is good to be with the monks. I have gone home. Can you really go home? Maybe Thomas Wolfe was right. Maybe you can't.

Who Did You Say I Was?

Because of my affection for the man that was a father figure for all of my monastic years, I visited Abbot Philip every time I returned to St. Gregory's.

During the last years of Philip's life, though he remained strong in body, he lost his memory. I would try to help him remember by asking, "Don't you recall that you were the abbot for nearly 20 years, that you gave me my name, George?" I wanted him to remember that I was his "good and faithful servant" for those years. I needed him to remember so I could feel better; yet he could not and would ask, "Who did you say I was?"

Nor could he recall that I was a good monk who instructed the young brothers, that I obediently got my MBA degree, that I had his confidence, was trusted by him. He could not fill the void that I had inside, nor assuage my sadness, nor help me heal. He was no longer mindful of who I was or who he was. He died in November of 2007, ending my expectation of him doing my work for me and forcing me to do so.

I can now finish my book. I have described my life as a monk, my experience with my "lady dragon," my leaving, and choices I have made to integrate my past with my present: Thesis-Antithesis-Synthesis. Time to move on.

The last time I was at the monastery, I no longer had tears to shed over the graves of my monastic brothers. On an unconscious level, I was reaching completion. I walked across the campus of what St Gregory's had become, a university with buildings that I had neither helped plan or build, a faculty, except for a few monks, that I didn't know.

A security guard approached me and asked, "May I help you find something, sir?"

I replied, far more prophetically than I realized, "No, I can find my own way."

I have been writing this book for many years and from a number of perspectives. First, it was about family therapy, then about relationships, and finally my own story with teachings garnered from my journey. A friend who has written many books told me that I would probably write only one. He, 'til now, was correct. I have written the final version and have reached an integration of my past into my present. This book has been *my* therapy.

I needed Abbot Philip to die for me to let go. The fear of letting go is something I have had to face. I did not trust that there was life for me after ending my old story. I played with the idea of titling my book, *What Do You Say After You Say Good-bye?* It is no mystery that this is the area of expertise I have developed in my profession as a psychotherapist. I have helped many people let go and say good-bye to the past and to relationships and helped them say hello to a new story for themselves, and not apply that to myself. Writing this book has done that for me.

My dreams have changed. For years I had confusing monastic dreams in which I failed at a monastic task or, as a priest, forgot the words while saying mass. I don't have these dreams anymore.

Here are two new dreams that indicate my letting go and my new story: I am standing in the monastic choir stalls with other monks practicing a Gregorian chant that requires concentration to sing in unison. I notice that my daughters Sarah and Jennifer are sitting at the end of the choir stalls. Because they are being disruptive, I sternly correct them and return to sing the chant. Noticing that they are hurt by my action, I leave the monks and go comfort my daughters.

Another dream: I am in a beautiful canyon. Abbot Philip is there, along with a small group of others. It is time for mass, and Abbot Philip is to be the celebrant. He begins to sing (he never sang on key). I notice a shaggy dog, the kind that stands about knee high and has hair covering his eyes. Strangely, but wonderfully, from inside the dog comes the sweetest music I've heard. The dog and I walk joyfully together down the canyon and away from the people.

When I awoke from both dreams, I felt complete.

Abbot Philip is dead. So is what was, wasn't, and might have been. Now, I am free to finish the book, live now, live fully now. I am looking forward to how the quality of my visit to the Abbey will be different the next time I return.

Unless my plans change, I will be buried in the monastic cemetery. My wife Carol said that she will drive (she doesn't like to fly) to St. Gregory's with my ashes.

She told me, "I don't want to go there directly. I want to enjoy my trip by traveling through Nevada, Utah, Colorado, then to Oklahoma. Maybe I will take the southern route through Arizona, New Mexico, then to Texas, and finally Oklahoma."

I replied, "That will be alright with me."

Epilogue – George and Lady Dragon: A New Myth

"Out beyond ideas of wrong doing and right doing, there is a field. I'll meet you there." Rumi

Fear, like a plague, permeated the land causing the villagers to feel so insecure that they constantly were on alert looking for a possible dragon attack. There had been sightings! The dragon was spotted in the dark and moist forest near the village. Old men told stories of their encounters with the enemy, saying that the creature came from the earth, snake-like, breathing fire and making a sound that froze a victim in his shoes or knocked him from his horse. These stories reminded the villagers of the serpent that tempted Eve in the garden-of-Eden. Maybe the dragon was another incarnation of Satan himself. Oh, how terrorized were the people of the village! Especially vulnerable were the defenseless maidens who were so pure and innocent and needed to be protected from the dragon. There were stories of maidens being abducted from the village and carried off into the darkness of the forest. No one knew for sure what nefarious act the dragon would perform on the holy innocents. Maybe they would be taken into that dark place, raped and killed.

Because of these fears, the village council voted to act preemptively. Better to attack than to wait for the dragon to slither into town and devour the innocent. They called upon the most famous dragon slayer of all to carry out this mission. George was a knight who had many successes in dragon extermination. He took up his lance and mounted his white horse, riding out into the forest. His mission was greatly supported by the people who viewed him as their savior.

As he rode, sitting high upon his horse, he could view the wild country that surrounded him. The vegetation became dense, there was less light, and the earth below oozed with moisture. He knew from past skirmishes how to find this creature of destruction. He looked for a crack in the earth that made it possible for the dragon to emerge from below. In his experience, dragons always come from below.

He arrived at a cave, a deep dark hole in the ground. He thrust his lance into the hole and heard a terrifying roar from inside. Suddenly the dragon, breathing fire, emerged to defend and attack. George, with shield in one hand and in the other a lance, was ready to pierce the underbelly of the creature, where the dragon was most vulnerable. Never before had George allowed himself to examine his prey. Why he did this time is still a mystery. He noticed, as the dragon moved forward to the mouth of the cave, that it was female. Not only her body announced itself as feminine, but she also spoke to him and he listened to her. She was Lady Dragon.

History was about to repeat itself! Throughout the ages George the dragon killer and Lady Dragon had engaged in familiar, predictable, safe, and painful combat. This battle continued to take place at the mouth of the cave out of which Lady Dragon would emerge. She had many forms in mythology. She, as Python, had defended Gaia, the earth goddess, from the arrows of Apollo. This day they (George and Lady Dragon) changed and began a new myth about their relationship. I believe it was Lady Dragon who gave the challenge to George. She asked what if both she and George could be more than their roles called for them to be?

Have you ever considered how much George was entrapped by his good guy image? Do you realize how difficult it is always to be virtuous and deny any behavior or feelings that do not fit? He must squelch any part of himself that might make him vulnerable. The dragon is the embodiment evil that must be eradicated. She is what must be avoided even though she attracts George. She is the temptress that represents everything not acceptable. This day George made the "mistake" of getting to know the enemy. He climbed off his white horse and listened to her as she told him what it was like to be Dragon Lady. She lamented that no one took her seriously as a force for good. She, though being very creative, was seen as earthy, the opposite of heavenly. She had been constantly entrapped into being the mysterious, dark force. She might be OK if she was soft and safe. Once she expressed her power, she was defined as strident, dangerous, scaly, and non-feminine. In that role she was the dangerous one who must he slain or at least kept under control.

George and Lady Dragon kept meeting outside the cave. They were very careful in their liaisons. George would come at night. His white horse was particularly visible if he came when there was light. So Dragon Lady could not illuminate the scene with too much fire. George would get off his horse, and the Dragon Lady lay beside him at the mouth of her cave. They would tell their life stories and explain how lonely it was being a paragon of virtue and evil. They told each other how envious they were of people who were not called to such perfection.

The cave reminded George of Mother Earth's womb from which he was being reborn. Because George slowly accepted dragon love into his heart, he explored his own earthy side and embraced it. Dragon acted as if she were more than serpent. She too, as a creative being, risked believing she was a heavenly creature as well. She acted as if she were as beautiful as the maidens in the village. This was especially possible as she received acceptance and love from George, and George from her. Through these trysts they learned quite a bit about each other and came away from them with a deeper knowledge, a forbidden knowledge.

Even though George by now was accomplished at embracing Lady Dragon, he struggled with accepting his own darkness. He still defined his perfection in terms of what he was to avoid in himself. To love himself as imperfect remained his daily practice. Lady Dragon needed the support to accept her beauty as a necessary component with her fiery power. She struggled with her paradox of softness and hardness, sensitivity and strength, compassion and power.

If their peers had known what was going on, George and Dragon Lady would have been rejected and maybe excommunicated. George would lose his place at the roundtable, and Lady Dragon would lose her place in the coven of dragons. So, you can understand how important it was to keep these meetings secret. At first they were very careful whom they would notify of their decision to be their integrated selves. George invited a few knights he knew and trusted to join him at the mouth of the cave. Dragon Lady invited some of her sisters whom she trusted. As they arrived, Lady Dragon and George encouraged them to take the same risks as they. Soon dragons and knights formed a conspiracy.

All continued to return to this place at the mouth of the cave, to thoroughly listen to one another, and to begin to change their lives. They thanked the Gods and Goddesses for the blessing of knowing good and evil. They were a community.

Becoming stronger in their solidarity, they began to meet in the daylight and would continue their celebration both in light and darkness. Many left their ordinary way of life. Some dragons decided not to go around scaring people anymore. Their hearts were no longer in that line of work. Criticism from their old community didn't frighten them the way it used to. Some dragons were rejected and excommunicated from the dragon society. The rejected dragons knew they were accepted by the conspiracy, and that mattered most. The knights shared similar experiences. Many lost their places at the roundtable of the king. Their losses were more than balanced by the love and acceptance of the conspirators.

These gatherings at the mouth of the cave were wondrous events. This place became so sacred to the conspirators that they felt free enough to be themselves, to be creative, and to experience the abundance that surrounded them as a community. One practice they had was storytelling. It was like a spiritual potluck. Someone would tell his or her story. Everyone present would thoroughly listen to what was said. Each would let the Word resonate inside, and share what that meant for him or her. In this way they united and tended to their community. They danced, sang, ate, and drank together. Some composed poems, wrote music, and conducted rituals commemorating the conspiracy.

*This myth calls us to **freedom**. It is an invitation to be who we truly are. Abandoning survival tactics generated by fear, we creatively enter Sacred Space where others of like spirit lovingly embrace us.*

# # #

Bibliography

Balistrieri, T.J. *PASSAGE (*Lecture Notes, *2004-2005).*
Bohm, David. *Wholeness and the Implicate Order.*
London and New York: Ark Paperbacks, 1983.
Bruteau, Beatrice, ed. *The Other Half of My Soul:*
Bede Griffiths and the Hindu-Christian Dialogue.
Wheaton, IL: Quest Books, 1996.
Everson, William. *Birth of a Poet.* Santa Barbara, CA:
Black Sparrow Press, 1982.
Gonzales Laurence. *Deep Survival: Who Lives, Who*
Dies, and Why. New York: W.W. Norton, 2004.
Goulding, Mary McClure and Robert L. Goulding.
Changing Lives through Redecision Therapy. New
York: Brunner Mazel, 1979.
Henry, Patrick, ed. *Benedict's Dharma: Buddhists*
Reflect on the Rule of St. Benedict. Translated by
Patrick Barry. New York: Riverhead Books, 2001.
Johnston, William. *The Still Point: Reflections on Zen*
and Christian Mysticism. New York: Harper & Row,
1970.
Kafka, Joe. *AIDS Victim Reflects on Life and Death,*
Indian Country News, October 22 1992.
McBrien, Richard P., ed. *The HarperCollins*
Encyclopedia of Catholicism. San Francisco:
Harper, 1995.
Merton Thomas. *The Asian Journal of Thomas*
Merton. New York: New Directions Books, 1973.
Willams, Terry Tempest. *Red: Passion and Patience in*
the Desert. New York: Random House, 2002.